MW01014140

THE EXPERIENCE

The **5** Principles of **Disney** Service and Relationship Excellence

BRUCE LOEFFLER AND BRIAN T. CHURCH

WILEY

CONTENTS

Part III

BACKSTAGE   225
(The Internal Interface)

FOREWORD

Few companies truly understand the value of creating a great customer Experience—and no organization has ever done it better than Disney. More than any other vocational encounter, Walt Disney World left an imprint in my mind and on my life. As one of the original cast members at Disney World in 1971, and during my 25 years as a member of the management team, creating an Exceptional Guest Experience was the foundation of our culture, as it still is today. We set out to build the "Happiest Place on Earth" and to design an Exceptional Experience like no other company in the world. I felt honored to be a small part of Disney's success.

"We work while others (our guests) play" was the motto we lived as we created a destination for guests around the world looking to escape their day-to-day routines for a world of fantasy, family, and fun. As a manager in the Merchandise Division for Walt Disney World and later the Disney University, it was part of my job to help instill the importance of building an incredible experience for our Disney guests through encouraging the idealism of service above expectation. I've long felt that someone needed to write a book and reveal the principles of excellence used to build an Exceptional Guest Experience . . . and now they have.

In 1983, a number of key leaders from across Walt Disney World united to form a team that was designed to take the Disney Experience to the next level. Within that team was a young man who created a new position to assist in enhancing the service and presentation skills of the Disney cast. His name was Bruce Loeffler. Since that time,

Bruce and I have worked on a number of projects while working at Disney as well as apart from Disney and have remained good friends over the past 30 plus years.

The principles presented in Bruce Loeffler and Brian Church's new book, *The Experience*, are an extension of many of the principles both Bruce and I taught during our years with Walt Disney World. What I found most beneficial in their book was the simplicity of the 5 "I. C.A.R.E." Principles. It is so important that companies and every person within those organizations understand how each individual is responsible for the "Impression" they create, the "Connection" that is formed, the "Attitude" they possess, their "Response" in the face of trials, and how well they deliver on the "Exceptionals" of serving their fellow cast members (employees).

As I read through the manuscript, I kept reflecting on each of the specific actionable steps that serve as a blueprint on how to develop a service culture, both on a personal level as well as professionally. *The Experience* is really a guide that is designed to take you and your organization to the next level of the Experience your company provides.

It is my pleasure to recommend *The Experience* to you. I encourage you to take some time to study it and determine how you can best apply it to meet your desired results. Bruce and Brian's desire is to help you determine where your company currently stands and how to apply the Principles in this book to achieve the next levels of service for your customers and clients. My congratulations to both Bruce and Brian for their creation of this helpful tool, and I thank them for their continued efforts in making service and the guest Experience a primary component of corporate culture.

Dr. Spencer Craig
Former Manager of Disney University and
the Walt Disney World Merchandise Division

ACKNOWLEDGMENTS

The level of effort that went into this book was staggering, and we certainly did not do it alone. We want to begin by thanking God from whom all ideas flow. We would like to thank our wives for putting up with our wild ideas and for sharing the vision to create *The Experience* book. A special "thank you" to Danielle Wingate for her help on spearheading the development of the tools that have helped to make this project so unique.

The work that you see before you was not without heavy collaboration from our writing coach, Jonathan Street. His skill certainly helped round out the special nature of this book. We would like to thank Ariel Benjamin for being our Director of Research and for captaining our team of Vanderbilt University students. The testing and researching of 500 companies could not have been done without their enormous efforts.

We want to thank Dr. Spencer Craig for his insight, stories, and direction. They called Spencer "Mr. Inspiration" at Disney, and he has certainly been an inspiration to both of us on the project.

We also would like to recognize Joe Scarlett for taking the time to share insights from Tractor Supply, one of the country's true masters of the customer Experience. Joe's stories, ideas, and insights led to many of the supporting ideas within the manuscript.

There are just too many people to acknowledge in this small section. We want to thank everyone who was pivotal in making the manuscript and this tool possible. You know who you are, and we humbly thank you for being a part of this awakening and for sharing our commitment to a customer-relationship- and service-based revolution.

Part I
Preshow (Setting the Stage)

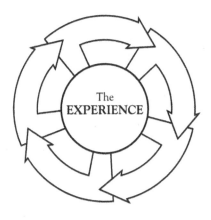

Chapter One
The Experience Path

Why We Wrote the Book and How to Use It

Disneyland will never be completed. It will continue to grow as long as there is imagination left in the world.

—Walt Disney

We set out to write *The Experience: The 5 Principles of Disney Service and Relationship Excellence* in an effort to engage the marketplace in its greatest area of need: the Experience for the frontline consumer. While my career has focused on relationship building, relational inflection points, and relationship momentum, I am now blessed to be able to collaborate with one of the finest customer service trainers in the world in Bruce Loeffler. Bruce spent more than 10 years working within the walls of Disney and several years as its Coordinator of Service Excellence. We have now combined our collective travels, experiences, and intellectual property to deliver this manuscript to you. We invite you to use this book as a tool for creating "Ambassadors" through Exceptional customer service and by building relational Experiences.

The book's second chapter presents the "I. C.A.R.E." Principles that you can use to test yourself, your services, and your organization using the Experience Quotient^{TM}. The idea was to create a path for you and your organization to achieve the Exceptional. Therefore, the book has been separated into three parts:

1. "Preshow"—for the book's overall idea, path, and premise
2. "Onstage"—for the ingredients to create an Exceptional Experience for your customers
3. "Backstage"—for the Experience created behind the scenes in leadership and for employees

We have carefully choreographed a blueprint for you to pontificate on the Principles; to use our Non-Negotiables and Quotient Questions to challenge yourself, to be supported by our Actionables; and then finally to test your company via our website (www.ExperienceQuotient .com) to see exactly what level of Experience you are providing.

We have spent an enormous amount of time testing a model that we believe provides the key to unlocking customer satisfaction, repeat business, and new customer growth. This book will allow you to advance methodically up the levels of the Experience hierarchy while gaining insight and specific details as to what the customer is seeking— and how to deliver it.

If you are interested in a beautifully choreographed concert of tactics that ends with a deliverable and an Experience for your customers, we encourage you to engage in the One Level Challenge at the end of this book. This is your personalized path to increasing the quality of the Experience you provide and, as a result, converting loyal customers into Ambassadors of your brand. We are excited to be your guides along this path.

Why Ambassadors?

You might be wondering why we have chosen the term *Ambassadors*. In 1815, the Congress of Vienna officially recognized ambassadors as having extensive powers to control the flow of information, maintain diplomatic relations, and project the influence of their chief executives. The word *ambassador* comes from the Medieval Latin words *ambactia* and *ambactiare*, which mean to "go on a mission." This "mission" is what happens when we cultivate an Experience that is valued and shared both internally and externally. In short, we are empowering others to be conduits to the magic and to go out and share the story.

Just as we need ambassadors for our national diplomacy, organizations need them to speak on behalf of the Experience. The issue is that these Ambassadors have to be developed. While people often share negative experiences on a regular basis, your customers and Ambassadors will share only positive Experiences of a certain level. Hence the purpose of this book: to empower you to deliver a higher level of the Experience.

Today's Ambassadors come in all forms. Many of them are consumers who like to share the experiences they have had with your product, company, or service. Some are employees who proudly carry the flag of the company and have a vested interest in your success. But they all share one thing in common: they are ordained to evangelize the world for your endeavors.

Why Disney?

It's no secret that the Walt Disney Company is the most recognized company in the world for the Experience and level of service excellence it provides. In fact, there is virtually no company on earth that connects people better to fun, enjoyment, happiness, fulfillment, service, and pure joy than the Disney Company. We have taken our eyewitness account of the service and relationship excellence at Disney to develop a model that was built to reflect and honor the hard work of Walt and Roy Disney, Dick Nunis, Van France, and the other founding fathers of Disney. In doing so, we considered important questions such as:

- What is it about Disney that differentiates its parks and their people from every other theme park—and truly, every other business—on the planet?

- What if your company could channel the excitement, develop the people, instill the principles, and get every employee engaged in the same way Disney does? What difference would it make in your business?

- What makes Disney so unique?

The answer to each of these questions is very simple: Disney creates an Experience unlike any other in the world, and its customers love it. Nearly every company we researched during our study has a desire to provide the service and create the impression that consumers experience within the walls of Disney; however, very few have been able to replicate it.

In the following pages, we define the five I. C.A.R.E. Principles that differentiate Disney from the typical service-oriented company. Our goal in creating these Principles—as well as our Experience Quotient tool—was to make our model applicable in virtually every industry that relies on a service offering or a service-oriented product to gain customers. Together, these tools act as a guide on how to intentionally and repeatedly deliver excellence for anyone or any entity that desires to provide an exceptional Experience. We want to enable *your* people to become true internal Ambassadors of the Experience, thus creating external Ambassadors out of their customer base who are committed to sharing their Experience with others.

Disney is not the only organization that we have studied that has mastered the Experience. We will discuss a few examples of other great American companies throughout the book. Whether it is Tractor Supply or Starbucks in retail, the Mayo Clinic for hospitals, the Four Seasons in the hotel industry, or even Southwest Airlines in transportation, they all have one thing in common: these companies, along with the Disney Corporation, possess a relentless resolve to creating the best Experience possible for their clients and customers. And they are all currently executing their Experience on an exceptional level.

The recipe is simple; but execution is the key. The first step is being committed to causing a certain level of the Experience. The second step is the execution thereof, as it is the actual Experience delivered that will empower and entice others to share their findings with the world. This journey is an investment into the development of the relational interface and service expectations of each phase of your business or entity. Get ready for what we believe is going to be a groundbreaking endeavor supported by years of fieldwork, empirical evidence, and a path for creating an unforgettable, repeatable, and shareable *Experience*!

Chapter Two
The "I. C.A.R.E." Principles

We've got to take care of these people. Honestly, Walt, we've got to expand Fantasyland. We've got to expand this park.

—Dick Nunis

As we identify in our research of more than 500 U.S.-based organizations, over 60 percent of service throughout the country is average or worse—both of which are unacceptable.

To be very blunt, service across the United States stinks. *As we identify in our research of more than 500 U.S.-based organizations, over 60 percent of service throughout the country is average or worse—both of which are unacceptable.* The disparity between good and poor service shows a total disconnect and disrespect for who the customers are and the fact that these individuals pay our salaries. That is why our idea of *Toxic service* is such a powerful concept—because we finally have a descriptive and appropriate term to define it.

Our research considered the caliber of service at several of the largest organizations in the United States—and we found that most consumers are less than impressed with the Experiences they're having. These organizations may have their business models down to a science, but their customer service model is inconsistent at best, and nonexistent at worst. Smaller companies—or as we call them, the Family 500—are a bit better at pleasing their customers than the Fortune 500. *According to a 2011 American Express survey, 80 percent of Americans agreed that smaller companies place a greater emphasis on customer service and the Experience than larger companies. Despite this data, smaller companies and closely held businesses still have a sizable gap in what organizations believe they are providing and what they actually deliver.*

We've titled the *solution* to the problem these companies face the "I. C.A.R.E." Principles, of which there are five in total. The first four deal directly with the Experiential interface with the consumer, customer, and client, while the fifth and final directly addresses the Experience you create internally for employees. Each Principle is supported by 10 sub-Principles that we call our "Non-Negotiables" that are meant to provoke thought and provide detail into the specific attributes of an exceptional Experience.

> *According to a 2011 American Express survey, 80 percent of Americans agreed that smaller companies place a greater emphasis on customer service and the Experience than larger companies. Despite this data, smaller companies and closely held businesses still have a sizable gap in what organizations believe they are providing and what they actually deliver.*

We will examine both sides of the organization's internal makeup: the Experience for the customer as well as the empowered Experience for employees. Some may ask: why both sides? Study after study on behavioral science in the workplace shows that employees who feel their leader genuinely cares about them as a person and makes the effort to invest in them are far more likely to deliver enhanced service, have a better attitude, and get along with each of their coworkers. Happy employees tend to be long-term employees. These are the people who become your *champions* and the ones you can convert into Ambassadors.

As Walt Disney himself once said, "What you do behind the curtain will eventually end up onstage." There is more to the Experience than simply the interface with the consumer. The Experience that an organization is committed to causing for its clientele must begin with the Experience that the organization is committed to causing for its own people.

Do You Care?

With the framework of *The Experience*, you will find the opportunity to invest in the personal growth, the value, and the role that each employee plays in the success of the company. Succinctly stated, our most important "customer" should be the frontline person who actually serves the customer. If we do not take good care of our frontline staff, they have little incentive to provide any better service to their paying customer than the way they were treated. After all, the way the staff is treated is the way that they will treat your guests in your absence.

With regard to the overall Experience created by your organization, it is incumbent upon every employee, manager, and executive to (1) know where they stand, (2) know where they want to be, and (3) have a plan and a process to help them improve. *The Experience* book, the "I. C.A.R.E." Principles, and the Experience Quotient offer a path and the advice to help you do exactly this.

Defining the 5 "I. C.A.R.E." Principles

I. ~ Impression: The lasting imprint made through first and ongoing relational inflection points; the catalyst to building a relationship.

(continued)

(*Continued*)

C. ~ Connection: The pivot point between contact and relationship. Converting clients and customers from consumers to Ambassadors (those on a mission to tell the world specifically about you) hinges on the ability to create the cerebral, emotional, and personal Connection.

A. ~ Attitude: The filter for everything you think, say, and ultimately do. Attitude is the lens through which you see the world and the outward expression of inward feelings.

R. ~ Response: Service is about personal responsibility and responding as opposed to reacting. The hallmark of customer service and an exceptional Experience is the Response. If the Response time, tone, and talent do not match up with every other aspect of an exceptional Experience, everything else is rendered useless.

E. ~ Exceptionals: The secret behind the Experience is the relational expertise and execution that come from the people in charge of delivering it. The management team and employees must be prepared, empowered, and endowed to have the Experience living and breathing within them.

This book is a tool that creates Ambassadors of the Experience, and defines the five I. C.A.R.E. Principles that differentiate Disney and other fine organizations from their competition. What we believe is most unique about this book is that it is applicable in virtually every industry where a service deliverable is essential to the success of the organization. Our book is built to enable your people, leaders, and organization to be much more successful, creating one dynamic, focused, and practical solution to what companies are missing today: an exceptional Experience.

So—let's get started.

Chapter Three
Five Levels of the Experience

What Level Are You?

The purpose of life is to experience the utmost, to reach out eagerly and without fear for a richer and newer experience.

—Eleanor Roosevelt

Customer service is worse today than it has ever been. Our internal research tells us that customers are increasingly frustrated because they feel that "no one seems to care." What is truly sad is that it takes no more time to be warm, friendly, and personable than it does to go through the motions. Where has the genuine care gone? Where is the relentless resolve to cause an exceptional Experience?

Every person wants to feel important—and every consumer has a choice of where to do business. If a particular organization does not provide better service or a better Experience than what a consumer can receive over the Internet, why would a customer make the effort to come into the restaurant, store, or other establishment? Consumers want and deserve to feel valued, welcomed, and as if they really matter. Today's technology and social media capabilities give them the power to positively or negatively affect your brand. The Experience you deliver therefore has an enormous impact on your bottom line.

Research shows that today's customers are not just disappointed or dissatisfied; they are outraged. *Reporter Brad Tuttle's article in* Time *magazine of June 7, 2011, entitled "Customer Service Hell" tells us that while 80 percent of companies believe that they* provide *superior customer service, only 8 percent of clients feel that they* receive *superior service from these same companies.* This highlights a tremendous opportunity for businesses that desire to gain a real competitive advantage. *A 2010 Customer Experience Impact Report by Harris Interactive stated that 9 out of 10 customers would pay more to ensure a superior customer experience.* If these businesses were to provide a great experience for their customers when their competitors are providing a lousy one, they would not only be different, they'd be superior.

> *Reporter Brad Tuttle's article in* Time *magazine of June 7, 2011, entitled "Customer Service Hell" tells us that while 80 percent of companies believe that they* provide *superior customer service, only 8 percent of clients feel that they* receive *superior service from these same companies.*

> *A 2010 Customer Experience Impact Report by Harris Interactive stated that 9 out of 10 customers would pay more to ensure a superior customer experience.*

The stores we've come to know as big box retailers are losing customers by the droves. And most fail to recognize that their inability to create a positive experience is the problem. Unless we fix the holistic service problem—the total Experience—businesses will continue to see a steady decline in customers and therefore in revenue.

What Level Are You On?

As mentioned in Chapter 2, our independent study of more than 500 U.S. organizations found that more than 60 percent of all customer service provided in America is average or worse *(Toxic)*. Consumers are tired of paying for mediocrity that could easily be improved with a modicum of effort on the part of leaders and employees who care. We have discovered that every store, supermarket, car dealership, hospital, fast-food restaurant, hotel, airline, financial advisory firm, bank, and church fits into one of five levels of the Experience hierarchy.

As mentioned in Chapter 2, our independent study of more than 500 U.S. organizations found that more than 60 percent of all customer service provided in America is average or worse (Toxic).

Every executive, every manager, and every employee needs to clearly understand what level of service and Experience their organization provides and why. Once they have identified the what and the why, the next step is to develop a plan of action to take their service and business to the next level. It is not a quick fix or an easy problem to rectify, but that is precisely what *The Experience* book was built to help you do.

Motel "X"

The average person with a complaint will tell roughly 16 others of their frustration—a domino effect that has only been magnified by current technology. Nowadays, a customer's power to positively or negatively affect a brand or an organization has enhanced the importance of positive Ambassadors as critical to those organizations' success, viability, and sustainability.

The average person with a complaint will tell roughly 16 others of their frustration—a domino effect that has only been magnified by current technology.

Several years ago, Bruce was taking his young daughter to church one Sunday morning. They were about halfway there when his daughter informed him that she had to use the bathroom. So Bruce quickly pulled off the road and into a Motel "X."

He politely asked, "Could my daughter use your restroom?" The young lady at the front desk said, "I'm sorry, but no." Bruce asked again: "It's an emergency; she really needs to use the bathroom." To which the clerk replied, "It's a company policy that nonguests cannot use our restroom." At this point, Bruce demanded that she get a manager. The clerk went in the back for 20 seconds and returned, telling him, "He said it is our company policy; you cannot use our restroom!" Bruce was annoyed, but figured there wasn't much else he could say or do—so he left.

Although the scenario didn't end in disaster, Bruce did write a letter to the CEO of Motel "X" and asked a simple question: "Is it true that a nonguest cannot use your restrooms?" A week later he received this reply: "Dear Mr. Loeffler, we're sorry for your inconvenience. When your travel plans call for lodging, please use Motel X"—along with a stamped signature. Bruce was not very impressed, so he wrote a second letter—a little stronger this time—stating three things:

1. You didn't answer my question.

2. I didn't appreciate your form letter.

3. Do not send me any more stamped signatures!

This was the response to his second letter:

Dear Mr. Loeffler, If you will look on page 175 of the Motel "X" directory, you will find the answer to your problem.

—along with another stamped signature.

Of course, they didn't send him a Motel "X" directory or a copy of page 175. So two of Bruce's students at Texas Christian University went to a Motel "X" and brought in copies of the directory. And what do you know? Page 175 said *nothing* about a nonguest not being able to use the Motel "X" restroom.

Motel "X" sent Bruce form letters, failed to answer his question, and provided him with stamped signatures—and after all of this, it turns out they'd lied to him. By this time, Bruce was very unimpressed with Motel "X"; so he decided to write a much stronger third letter. By this point, they must have thought they had a wild man on their hands—so they decided to call Bruce back this time.

A vice president named Bill called and said, "Mr. Loeffler, you need to understand that we don't treat our customers like this." To which Bruce responded, "Oh, yes, you do—otherwise we wouldn't be having this conversation!" Bill replied, "Well, I'd like to resolve this today." Bruce then answered, "You can't. It's too late for that. Either I get a phone call or a letter from your CEO or this will go on indefinitely."

Ten days later, Bruce received a one-page, single-spaced letter with a real-life signature from the CEO of Motel "X," who profusely apologized by saying, "This is the first time I have been made aware of your situation." Bruce replied, "I knew that; but the people below were misrepresenting and, in this case, lying about Motel X's policies."

Now let's return to the statement we made at the beginning of this story. The average person with a complaint will tell how many people about it? Roughly 16.

Therein lies the power of word of mouth advertising. Up to this point, Bruce has told more than 160,000 people of his Motel "X" experience (using the real company name!). Let's apply this principle, and *you* go out and tell 10 of *your* friends. Those 10 friends were each going to spend two nights at Motel "X" over the next year at $50 per night, but now have decided *not* to. Here is the potential lost revenue for Motel "X":

$$160,000 \text{ (told about the Motel "X" experience through Bruce's seminars)}$$

$$\underline{\times \ 10} \text{ (the friends they will tell)}$$

$$= 1,600,000 \text{ (potential lost customers)}$$

$$\underline{\times \ \$100} \text{ (what they would potentially have spent)}$$

Total
Potential $= \$160,000,000$
Loss

That's $160 million in potential lost revenue—because they wouldn't let one little girl use their restroom. Now, one day those 160,000 people will turn into 200,000, and then will become 300,000—and then when Bruce's third book comes out, more than a half million people will have been told about this incident.

This example clearly shows how critical the Experience is even to those who are not current paying customers. The Experience that we are committed to and are designing for others must be genuine; it shouldn't be something we can turn on and off like a light switch. If it's real, and the "magic is magic," it will not only help you build a more successful service deliverable; it just may save you millions.

The Staggering Results

In the following diagram, you will see the breakdown of our 500+ company study and the model of the five levels of the Experience. We took select service-oriented companies from the Fortune 500 along with the aforementioned Family 500 (closely held small businesses). Our findings are described in the box.

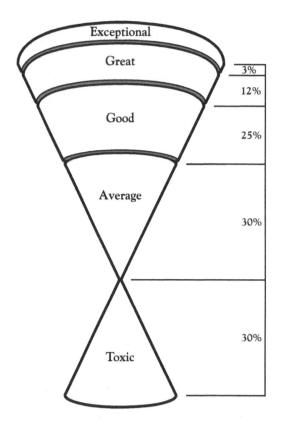

The Five Levels of the Experience

LEVEL ONE (TOXIC): 30 PERCENT

L1 Defined: "Service that comes across as apathetic, indifferent, and disengaged while providing an Experience that is both impersonal and offensive."

The definition we've developed for "Toxic" is that *the service provided actually offends and frustrates the customers.* In simplified

(continued)

(Continued)

terms, Toxic means negative employee attitudes. It includes reactions and interactions involving apathy, the brush-off, and plastic indifference. This is by far the lowest level of service Experience; it's clear that people do not care and leaders are unaware they are losing customers and risking going out of business.

LEVEL TWO (AVERAGE): 30 PERCENT

L 2 Defined: "An Experience where employees are content to go through the motions, are satisfied with the status quo, and deliver service that is mediocre, bland, and uninspiring."

Although not as negative as "Toxic," the level of "Average" is still unacceptable. These companies are out of touch with customers' needs. Average is neither good nor bad; it just *is*. Companies and individuals who provide average or mediocre service tend to be uninspiring and boring in their delivery. Would a caring parent tell a child, "I want you to strive to be a C student"? Average may be tolerable to some, but it is unacceptable if you desire excellence.

LEVEL THREE (GOOD): 25 PERCENT

L 3 Defined: "Service where employees are often engaged, friendly, and personable, where most customers or clients encounter a positive Experience and feel as though they are valued, welcome, and important."

In our opinion, the level of "Good" is where every company, leader, and employee needs to begin, at a minimum. Levels One and Two make up roughly 60 percent of all service;

(continued)

(*Continued*)

but that 60 percent is not at all acceptable *if* you want to succeed. This third level of Good provides the foundation for building excellence in an organization. Everything about Good helps define where every company must start, realizing that anything below Good will not be tolerated.

LEVEL FOUR (GREAT): 12 PERCENT

L 4 Definition: "Relational Service that is consistently strong, where employees go the extra mile to create personalized service and relational Experiences for every customer."

"Great" is the fourth level of the Experience, reserved for companies and individuals who tend to go out of their way for their customers. They create a great atmosphere for employees and design a legacy of excellence in everything they do. They tend to have a completely different mindset, excellent attitudes, and a high level of engagement, and strive to differentiate themselves from the competition.

LEVEL FIVE (EXCEPTIONAL): 3 PERCENT

L5 Definition: Exceptional Service that is part of the show, where every employee is focused on creating a unique 'Experience' for each customer that is profoundly better than their competition.

This top level of the Experience is reserved for the truly "Exceptional" companies that tend to take service to a whole new level. They create a memorable and unique experience and, by doing so, develop Ambassadors who spread the word to the world every chance they have.

Why Are the Levels Important?

We are only as good as our reputation—and we are often only as profitable in our ventures as the level of new and repeat customers that we garner. To grow our organizations and from a cost efficiency perspective, we must focus on three things:

1. Keeping our current customers

2. Creating a wave of repeat business

3. Gaining new clients and customers via referral or word of mouth

The most effective way to do this is to create loyal customers, convert them into Ambassadors, and then empower these Ambassadors to share their Experience with others. Understanding the Five Levels of the Experience—and, more important, where *you* rank—is crucial to your organization. There are only certain levels of the Experience where Ambassador conversion takes place.

We found in the independent study we conducted that people who came into contact with Level Four (Great) and Level Five (Exceptional) organizations were the only ones who were willing to tell their spheres of influence about their positive Experience. Driving home the importance further, *we found that Level Five Ambassadors were nearly twice as willing to share their stories as Level Four customers. The flip side of the coin was that more than 70 percent of the people who came into contact with Level One (Toxic) and Level Two (Average) organizations went out of their way to share their negative experiences with their spheres.*

> *We found that Level Five Ambassadors were nearly twice as willing to share their stories as Level Four customers. The flip side of the coin was that more than 70 percent of the people who came into contact with Level One (Toxic) and Level Two (Average) organizations went out of their way to share their negative experiences with their spheres.*

We know that the stakes are incredibly high given the intense competition in most industries multiplied by the ability for customers to affect a brand positively or negatively. This has rendered commitment to service excellence non-negotiable. You must provide a competitive level of the Experience focused toward the Exceptional; otherwise your organization will eventually be in jeopardy. You can move up only one level at a time—but the goal is ultimately to be at Level Four (Great) or Level Five (Exceptional) to convert clients into brand Ambassadors.

Now What?

Our desire and goal was to design an Experience model that would be congruent with that of the known business world's accepted service excellence standard of Disney. We then wanted to be able to test our model against any organization's current level of the Experience. However, it's not enough to be able to test. We wanted our readers to have a set of Principles to go by, to have Quotient Questions to challenge them, and to have Actionables to coach them. Finally, we wanted them to have a clear road map to follow that would allow them to move up the levels of the Experience.

Warning: Do not try to utilize all of the Actionables at once; that is not the way this book was set up or how this tool works. Take the Experience Quotient test at www.ExperienceQuotient.com and utilize the feedback and advice to work on your weaknesses and threats. You will soon find yourself and your organization on the path to the exceptional Experience and, as a result, converting your clients and customers to lifelong Ambassadors.

Part II
Onstage (The Customer Interface)

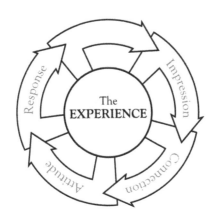

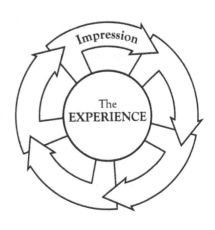

Chapter Four
Principle 1: Impression

Disneyland is a show!

—Walt Disney

Every customer has an *Impression* of every encounter experienced, and can describe and file each of these Impressions under one of three classifications: positive, negative, or neutral. Though "neutral" might seem like the absence of an Impression, it is every bit as critical as "positive" or "negative." It says that the company did nothing to distinguish its service or itself from its competitors. Average never inspired anyone. The individuals and the companies who provide indifferent or mediocre service leave the Impression that you are simply not important enough to them.

The Impression is so important because it is the epicenter that drives every inflection of the customer relationship. Every time a customer has any type of contact with any aspect of your business, the customer forms an opinion. *If you research behavioral science, you*

> *If you research behavioral science, you know that opinions usually result in actions. Impressions form opinions, and opinions form actions, whether positive or negative, purchase or pass, or return with family or never visit again.*

know that opinions usually result in actions. Impressions form opinions, and opinions form actions, whether positive or negative, purchase or pass, or return with family or never visit again.

Impressions are often driven by an organization's culture: who we are, what we stand for, and how much we care. As the saying goes, "People don't care how much you know until they know how much you care." Impressions are the template of how much an organization and its people really care. Disney has become the expert at creating exceptional Impressions at every juncture of the Experience at a Disney theme park. And its secret, from the painted cement symbolizing a red carpet at the entrance to the warm and friendly smiles at exit, is an unflagging resolve to cause the best Experience possible for its guests.

Intentional Impressions

Disney operates according to the maxim that virtually everything the public or the customer sees must be choreographed and finely tuned. This is why about 90 percent of everything a cast member (employee) at any Disney park does is planned, scripted, and well rehearsed. What Disney is creating—and what your organization must realize—is that it is part of the bigger picture, or, as Disney would call it, part of the show. Every successful "show" and every successful company is a success primarily because it is designed to be a success. We get into trouble when we leave things to chance or are ill prepared.

Think of a Broadway play or musical. How does the cast and crew put on the same show, night after night, year after year, and keep it *consistently exceptional* every performance? They do it by selecting the right people, setting standards of performance, training repeatable skills, and expecting levels of consistent excellence in every encounter, every time. Creating positive Impressions of your business is no different than a Broadway show or Walt Disney World.

Bruce, who was with Disney for more than 10 years, had the privilege of being part of the performing group, "Kids of the Kingdom" that performed in front of Cinderella's Castle in the hub at Walt Disney World. The show lasted 25 minutes. Prior to ever performing, the cast would rehearse and rehearse and rehearse in the Production Center day after day. One day Bruce calculated how much time was spent rehearsing. He was surprised to discover that they rehearsed *seven hours for each minute* they were onstage. The key is to develop people to become professionals who can demonstrate repeatable skills on a consistent basis. This means that Impressions are both the natural and repeatable skills that we train and expect our people to deliver on a consistent basis.

The Differentiator

Those individuals and the companies that are different, better, and unique are this way because they're able to differentiate their people from their competitors'. Consider a typical bank, for instance. All banks and financial institutions are heavily regulated by the U.S. government. In essence, there is virtually no difference between Bank A, Bank B, and Bank C other than a few basis points here or there. This means that the only *real* difference is in the Experience and the people. The attitudes, level of service, and personalization they provide are what create or destroy the Experience—and are the ultimate differentiator.

Whether banking, retail, or a theme park, the commitment to service excellence and not pricing is what sets an organization apart. While spending time with Joe Scarlett, former CEO of Tractor Supply, and a few of the good people on the front lines there, I was informed of a sign that hangs above every checkout counter that reads, "All team members have the authority to do what it takes." This is the mindset and the commitment to doing what most people and most organizations are simply not willing to do. It's different!

Impressions—and our ability to create them—are one of the most powerful tools we have at our disposal. Every day, often without realizing it, we create lasting Impressions of ourselves and the organizations we work for. Those first impressions have the ability to either make us or break us in the minds of our customers. Impressions leave an indelible imprint that will form an opinion that is stronger than steel.

Impression: Ten Disney-Inspired Non-Negotiables

Impression 1.1: Engage
The first Impression! Engaging and making the effort for initial positive contact.

Impression 1.2: Intentional
Establishing your positive intentions up front and then providing excellent service on purpose.

Impression 1.3: Senses
Impressions are connected and driven by the five senses (sight, scent, sound, taste, and touch).

Impression 1.4: Emotion
Examining emotion as the sixth sense and why it is important.

Impression 1.5: Presentation
Preparation and repetition in the show we call business.

(continued)

(Continued)

Impression 1.6: **Professionalism**

From appearance to greetings, this aspect echoes in the minds of consumers.

Impression 1.7: **Pristine**

From the outside as well as inside the facility and including personal appearance, this point is extremely important to the Experience.

Impression 1.8: **Pride**

The centerpiece of service standards.

Impression 1.9: **Likeability**

The art and science of treating everyone like a guest.

Impression 1.10: **Consistency**

The secret to acquiring Ambassadors who will share their Experience.

Impression 1.1:
Engage

In motivating people, you have to engage their minds and their hearts.

—Rupert Murdoch

First Impressions are the lifeblood of any relationship. The initial engagement is the catalyst and the most crucial relational inflection point for new or potential customers. Close your eyes and think back to a terrible first engagement you had somewhere like a hotel or a restaurant. Was it the disheveled look of the valet attendant? Was it the potholes in the driveway? Was it the attitude of the waiter or the person on the phone taking the reservation? Now think of one of the greatest first impressions you have ever encountered. Was there a smile and a presence that you just could not explain with words—one that drew you in and made you feel at home?

In his book You Are the Message *(Doubleday, 1989), author Roger Ailes maintains that we formulate first impressions in the first seven seconds of an interaction.* We are often evaluated by others in a few moments based on our appearance, body language, tone of voice, hair style, attitude, facial expressions, shyness or confidence, personality, accent, and a multitude of other Impressions we project in the initial minutes if not seconds of meeting someone new.

We are not merely trying to impress people; rather, what we do, how we do it, how we act, and what we say all leave an indelible impact on everyone with whom we come in contact. This notion holds true especially in brief encounters. Our research shows us that roughly 80 percent of the customer's interaction *with* you is based on their first impressions *of* you. It's also important to remember that the science of the first impression holds true not just with people but also in regard to products, venues, and services. Think of one of the products that you use every day. How about your telephone? Apple has built an empire out of creating Experiences with and through its products. Is your phone merely used for utility or tactical purposes, or does it do more? The Experience created through a product is derived through its usability, its special features, and the happiness created, and by generally improving the life or the moment for its user.

As overused as the saying "You never have a second chance to make a first impression" is, it is true. When we truly understand what is at stake here, we learn to treat the first Impression as if it is the only opportunity to set the tone for the relational Experience that we seek to cause. You must envision yourself as the only contact that the client, consumer, or visitor will ever have. It is now or never—you or no one. Execute properly, and you are able to initiate the entrée to the Experience you envision; execute poorly, and you'll thwart the Experience with almost no opportunity to salvage it.

Welcome

One of the most important actions any business can take initially is to acknowledge customers and make them feel welcome. This is the first opportunity to show that you are different, that they deserve better, and that you care. It may seem obvious, but we often do not remember that the objective is to create an Experience worthy of sharing—one that will compel customers to tell others how welcomed your business made them feel.

Making every customer feel genuinely welcome is one of the most important responsibilities you or your organization can ever encounter. That is why you will you will find a greeter outside virtually every attraction at the Disney parks. The greeter's primary job is to welcome guests and direct them where to go. Greeters also provide information, such as how long the wait time will be and what the attraction is all about. Although it may seem minor, their job is to create a positive first Impression each guest will have of the attraction and to set the tone for the Guest Experience.

Stand Out

What separates you from every other competitor? What makes you unique and different? What would be the response to consumers and prospective clients who ask, "Why would I want to choose you over the ABC Company?" It is often those subtle, small differences that separate you from the competition.

One of our favorite people is entrepreneur, author, and motivational speaker Jim Rohn, who is famous for saying that there are only about four or five very small differences between you and the competition. Merely tweaking and fine-tuning those four or five differences would therefore allow your company to become markedly better than your competition. In our opinion, there are five and we call them the I.C.A.R.E. Principles.

Take Starbucks for an example. The Starbucks brand difference is based on a few minor differences that, when combined, have formed a major delta in the overall Experience and the Impressions it delivers. Starbucks has converted their staff into experts and turned the verbiage and the expectations from those of fast-food employees to those of baristas and experts of the coffee Experience. The Seattle-based behemoth has created community in an industry that was previously viewed as an on-the-go beverage provider. Starbucks has become a place to meet and not merely a coffeehouse. Competitors are abundant, but Starbucks changed the game and made its Experience repeatable across the country en route to operating at more than 17,000 locations around the world today.

Make It About Them

Most initial engagements and first Impressions tend to be all about you and your execution. You ask yourself: Is the storeroom clean? Is the sign lit? How do I look? How is my smile and my posture? Is my breath okay? While that is exactly what you should be doing, the second Impression must be all about *them*. What do *they* want, need, and expect? And how you can best deliver it to them?

Human nature dictates that we focus on our presentation and how professionally we come across or present ourselves. As important as those two things are, you must remember the other part of the equation—the customer. A girl named Mary was dating two guys, Tom and Bob, both of whom she cared deeply about. A girlfriend asked, "So, is it Tom or is it Bob?" Mary replied, "Tom is so wonderful—he has so many great qualities." Excitedly, her girlfriend piped, "So you're going to marry Tom!" Mary said, "No. When I'm with Tom I feel like *he's* the most fun and the most exciting person in the room, but when I'm with Bob, he makes me feel like *I'm* the most important person in the world." Ultimately, it isn't about you; it's about them.

Quotient Question

How demonstrative and strategic are the efforts to make positive first Impressions with your clients or customers?

(*continued*)

(Continued)

Actionables

To the customer, *you* are the company. It is your job to initiate and create a positive first Impression with each customer you encounter.

Try this

☞ When first meeting a customer, be personable and friendly. Welcome them with a genuine smile, eye contact, and a warm greeting. Rehearse this with a coworker and contemplate having a daily warm-up for client- and customer-facing employees in the organization. We call it "engagement calisthenics."

Try this

☞ Before you start work each day, take a moment to look in the mirror and give yourself a big smile—just in case you forgot what it looks like. Next, try a frown, next anger, next confusion, and finally apathy. It is important for you to see what customers see every day and how it looks on you.

Try this

☞ Look every customer directly in the eye. The more genuine your warmth is, the more it reflects in your eyes as a smile. When you look customers in the eye, it demonstrates confidence in yourself and a primary reason to trust you. It's easiest to start with coworkers and in your own home. Build the eye contact habit and watch the level of how people Experience you increase.

Impression 1.2:
Intentional

The way to get started is to quit talking and begin doing.

—Walt Disney

How and how well we serve others must be deliberate. We must develop an intentional plan, purpose, and personality behind the service deliverable. Excellent companies differentiate themselves by setting expectations of the type of business and caliber of service they desire to embody. Then they make their intentions verbally and visibly known to their customers.

One of my favorite hotels is the Island Hotel, located on Fashion Island in Newport Beach, California. While the hotel has nice rooms and pleasant views, it is the service that is unprecedented. I would gladly pay a premium to stay there over other options. Not only do the employees always remember my name (not sure how they do that!), but they have a way of making it seem as if I am the only one who matters to them.

I can specifically recall one occurrence when I forgot a fishing license for a 5 a.m. expedition. I frantically called the hotel from the dock and took a cab back to the property. Upon arriving, I found that one of the employees had gone to the room (with my permission) and was at the entrance with the license and a cup of coffee made to my abnormally difficult liking. I said to him, "You guys have the best service in the country!" His response: "It is intentional, sir!"

Visual and Verbal

While the intent must be there in *action*, it is also very important that customers know in advance that they can expect great service and Exceptional Experiences. Upon checking into a Four Seasons hotel recently, Bruce and Brian heard the woman working at the front desk say, "It is our intent to make your stay with us a great one." Then she walked us to the lobby elevator and presented each of us with a key to our respective rooms. Now, you may not find this earth-shattering; but the little things make the biggest difference: the positive attitude, the way she prepared us for great service, and the way she supported it with immediate action.

Many things can go unnoticed, even if you are at the top of your game. There must be a consistent message embedded in your actions but also in verbal expectation with regard to the Experience. Communicating this regularly to the client base can have its downfalls as well. Consumers' expectations could become mismanaged if you don't support your words and messaging with authentic action. However, we truly believe the level of the effort and execution usually comes down to the level of expectation that is prevalent.

At Disney, there is such a high level of expectation from the consumer base that the Experience will be magical, that there is huge disappointment when there are holes in the Impressions created. The good news is that the holes are so irregular that they are easily seen, caught, and repaired by leadership and Ambassadors of the Experience. There is an important principle that states: employees will usually raise or lower their abilities in order to meet the consumers' expectations. That is, people naturally do exactly what they must, and little more. A great example of this is in the hotel industry. If the hotel is a budget hotel—and you can tell that from the road—and is for those who expect nothing more than a bed at a low price, that's all they will get. It's what the customer expects and it is all the employees will ever seek to deliver.

Many of us have the ability to raise our game or lower it in order to meet the level others anticipate from us.

Intentional

Intentional success requires that we develop a vision of where we want to be and how to get there. The Experience begins with our intentions to deliver the Exceptional. *Sadly enough, according to recent Forrester research, only 37 percent of leaders have a dedicated budget for customer Experience improvement initiatives.* Your efforts, your money, and your time must be dedicated to the Experience, or the best you can hope to deliver is an Average interaction. Every employee must be on board, and every leader must have a clear end result drawn up that is plainly communicated to every employee.

> *Sadly enough, according to recent Forrester research, only 37 percent of leaders have a dedicated budget for customer Experience improvement initiatives.*

Some Experiences are happenstance; others occur as a result of good luck or being at the right place at the right time. But most Impressions are and should be on purpose. The ingredients and the work that it takes to concoct an Experience that leaves an imprint and then compels someone to share it are not luck at all. They are intentional.

Quotient Question

How effectively are the efforts of positive service communicated up front to the customers, and are the employees intentional about delivering on the expectations?

(continued)

(*Continued*)

Actionables

Your responsibility is to intentionally create a positive, friendly place to visit by making each person feel welcome, valued, and important.

Try this

☞ Engage the 10-foot rule. Every time you come within 10 feet of customers or coworkers, smile, greet them, give them eye contact, and make them feel welcome.

Try this

☞ Ask clients and customers specifically about their day, comment on their attire or children, and offer suggestions to help them, to provide value, or to improve something.

Try this

☞ Build the "100 percent present muscles" through intentional acts of undivided attention. Practice this with your coworkers. Try making the customer feel as if he or she is the only person in the world. Don't let anything or anyone else distract you from your customer, especially your phone, your agendas, or your fatigue.

Impression 1.3:
Senses

Equipped with five senses, man explores the universe and calls the adventure Science.

—Edwin Powell Hubble

Disney World is a master at using the five senses. It employs individuals whose expertise focuses on how to best utilize sight, scent, sound, taste, and touch. Disney also studies virtually everything about guests' desires and habits. There is a reason why Disney uses yellows, reds, bright blues, and purples so often: because they are the warm colors. Consider the characters' clothing: Mickey's red pants, Minnie's purple bow, and Donald's blue coat. Inside the park, Disney has used these colors throughout the landscape. Through trial and error and expert color analysis, Disney has made a point to dress the park in happiness and incorporate the warm pigments from the color palette.

Can you remember back to when you were younger and had an epic evening with someone? Even though it has been 10, 20, or 30 years since the event, every time you smell that scent, hear that song, or see that place, a flood of emotions and memories brings you right back to that night. The senses and the triggers in your brain create some of the most powerful thoughts and memories you can draw on.

Sight

Many of us are impacted first and foremost by visual stimulation. What we see provides the first and most lasting Impression. Disney's excellent use of color and design to create the spectacular is one of many things that set it apart. The marketing department is usually the team that is most responsible for creating Disney magic through signage, brochures, and much of the artwork on display at each of the parks.

It shouldn't come as a surprise that retail stores appeal to your sense of sight first—especially when kids are targeted customers. If they can get you to purchase the brightest, latest, newest, or "I've gotta have it" toy, then they've done their job. What *is* surprising is the *way* they craftily entice guests to buy more and stay in the store longer. This concept works even for restaurateurs. Famed chef Giada De Laurentiis once said, "I'm into very colorful food. Obviously lots of flavor; but I think we eat with our eyes first, so it has to look great. The presentation has to be great."

The U.S. Department of Labor suggested in a recent study that 83 percent of human experiential learning is derived from sight. The remaining 17 percent is derived through the other senses—11 percent through hearing, 3.5 percent through scent, 1 percent to 1.5 percent through touch, and 1 percent by taste. Interior designers and executives in marketing and advertising know these statistics and take advantage of them. Experts in marketing know that certain colors tend to evoke distinct emotions. For instance, red is often used as a power color and tends to create conflict or action in people. Take the bull's-eye logo and trademark of Target. Can you imagine a target being any color other than red? A soft pastel or sky blue just doesn't evoke the same power and boldness.

Each area of each Disney theme park has aluminum trash cans painted specifically for that area. The themed trash cans are strategically placed 25 feet

> *The U.S. Department of Labor suggested in a recent study that 83 percent of human experiential learning is derived from sight. The remaining 17 percent is derived through the other senses— 11 percent through hearing, 3.5 percent through scent, 1 percent to 1.5 percent through touch, and 1 percent by taste.*

apart, because Disney has discovered that guests tend not to throw trash on the ground if there is a trash can within 25 feet. Even the streetlights are themed to fit each respective area. The goal is to have every aspect of a themed area not violate the integrity of the show in that area. What some may consider overboard, we consider the "art of the Impression."

Scent

One of Bruce's favorite tactics for appealing to a customer's senses was applied on Main Street at the Magic Kingdom. In the candy shop, there was a small room closed off by glass windows. The candy makers would often make peanut brittle in the room and guests could watch them through the glass. A special ventilation system was installed that pulled the fragrance from the room and sent it to an outlet on Main Street. Guests could smell peanut brittle a block away. That simple action quadrupled the sales of peanut brittle on Main Street when it was first put into action.

Scent is critical to your success as well. Our sense of smell connects customers to an emotional Experience. Receptors in the nose are able to detect thousands of smells each day and often help forge an emotional bond within the brain. As pleasant smells often create happy or positive memories, unpleasant odors can do just the opposite and repel customers. Nasty odors like fish, garbage, and even improperly cleaned bathrooms are a real turnoff to customers and can keep them from returning.

Smell is also very closely linked to memory. According to various studies, smell consistently is more accurate at stimulating a memory than a visual recollection. Much of what we smell has the power to quickly take us back to early memories. For example, when a former football player sets foot on a freshly cut athletic field, he is immediately transported back to his days on the gridiron. He gets a rush, dreaming of being able to go back in time to play one more game.

Sound (Hearing versus Listening)

People often have a moment when they ask themselves, "Did they hear me?" The real question behind this is: "Was this other person even listening?" The distinction here is definitely a matter of choice. *Hearing* is merely an involuntary process that starts with noise, vibrations, the movement of fluid in the ears, and sound sent to the brain. It gets a little complicated when the noise actually arrives at its final destination of the brain, since this is where *listening* happens.

Listening is a voluntary act where we try to make sense out of the noise we hear, whether it's your spouse telling you to run errands or your boss on your case about the latest sales figures. In any event, hearing and listening are very different because listening requires action on your part.

How does listening really happen? The four-step process is as follows:

1. **Hearing**—sound entering the eardrums and traveling to the brain
2. **Attending**—our brain receiving the sound and deciding what to pay attention to
3. **Understanding**—taking what is meaningful and applying it to the social context
4. **Remembering**—storing the information for use at a later time

For the most part, we have the process down pat (well, except for the remembering part). Viewers retain only a small percentage of what they hear on the evening news, and even with given clues, they still don't retain much more.

What does this all mean to you? In the derivation of an Experience, the objective is to have customers engaged to the extent that they are listening to your intent, your greeting, your instructions, and your excellence, not merely hearing.

Taste

With nearly 100 restaurants on Disney property, the sense of taste plays a large role in the Guest Experience. Especially at Epcot, variety is the order of the day. From the Biergarten in Germany to the Katsura Grill in Japan to the Nine Dragons Restaurant in China to Restaurant Marrakesh in Morocco and even the Liberty Inn at the American Pavilion, taste is paramount. Never underestimate the appetite of American consumers—and the attention to detail they give in their opinions on food quality and quantity.

A new company called Intentional Chocolate is taking the notion of the edible Experience to an entirely new level. It is utilizing a concept of "embedding good intentions," where there is a cerebral process of placing good thoughts and vibes into the ingredients before serving. According to the company's double-blind test at the University of Wisconsin, the researchers tested the well-being of consumers after partaking of Intentional Chocolate versus other forms of chocolate—and it works! The Intentional Chocolate improved the overall mood of the consumers by more than 67 percent over the normal chocolate sample. Whether it is meditation, prayer, or just extra care when preparing and delivering a meal, there is a credible reason to concentrate on the intentions and the Impressions that go into the food and drink within the Experience deliverable.

Touch

Walt Disney World is designed around the sense of touch and feel, which is used to gather and to convey information. For instance, a handshake in our culture reveals a lot of information to another person. A limp handshake denotes reluctance or lack of confidence, whereas a strong grip signifies confidence or control. The feel of the room or environment is very important. It's amazing what happens when the temperature of the movie theater, hotel room, or restaurant is too high or too low; it really has the power to kill the Experience, doesn't it?

What sets Disney apart is its ability to incorporate all five senses into the show and the service. We recognize that all five senses may not be completely applicable for every company, industry, or Experience. However, there are most definitely a few senses that are congruent with the Impressions you are trying to make—so it is imperative that you make those count.

Quotient Question

Where applicable, how well are the five senses (sight, scent, sound, taste, and touch) utilized to create a positive customer Experience?

Actionables

The more effective you are at utilizing each of the five senses, the more successful you will be at creating a memorable Impression.

Try this

☞ When you first meet a customer, look the part of a professional, and then practice matching the enthusiasm and confidence in your voice to the way you look. Look and sound the part. These two (sight and sound) are often the most noticeable and impressionable to the customer.

Try this

☞ Every customer has a hot button. Take notes and utilize technology to keep files on clients' or customers' likes, dislikes, and interests as quickly as possible and steer them toward their preferences. When you gain a feel for what they want, you can "touch" the customer cerebrally, leaving the desired Impression.

Try this

☞ Ask a customer and/or a friend to provide their honest opinion on what scent tells them about your business. Next, what do you need to do in order to enhance, change, or improve it?

Impression 1.4:
Emotion

Human behavior flows from three main sources, desire, emotion, and knowledge.

—Plato

Some call emotions the sixth sense. Emotions are powerful, as is the ability to positively influence the emotions of others. Advertisers and companies have long made an effort to capitalize on the emotions of consumers as they promote their products and services. Sir Richard Branson once said, "I've never been particularly good at numbers, but I think I've done a reasonable job with feelings. And I'm convinced that it is feelings—and feelings alone—that account for the success of the Virgin Brand in all of its myriad forms." Emotions evoke memories, and memories influence action—often to repeat the past, thus creating loyalty and an affinity for specific brands and services.

Emotion and Influence

Humans tend to be relational creatures. Most of us tip the scales on the side of either emotions or logic, and rarely give equal weight to both. Consequently, companies spend billions of dollars each year to reach our heartstrings through ads about dreams, wants, and aspirations that play on our emotions. Neurologist Donald Caine stated, "The essential difference between emotion and reason is that emotion leads to action while reason leads to conclusions." In simple terms, emotion plays on the heart while logic is all about the brain and reasoning things out.

45

In other words, emotion says, "I want this," while logic counters, "Why do I need this?"

We tend to connect to one of the two sides. It is often emotion that connects the consumer to a particular brand—quite frankly, if for no other reason than we want to take a break from reason and do what just feels good!

Disney is a master at creating emotion through its commercials, attractions, shows, fireworks, and service. It is very clear that everything that Disney does is focused and intentional on building relationships and creating emotional action. Disney creates emotions of "What am I missing?" "I can't wait to get back there," and "We've earned it . . . we deserve it!" These emotions often end in actions and thoughts of "I'm going to tell everyone about my Experience" and "I'm buying everything with 'Disney' on it!"

Emotion in the Value Proposition

Some companies have been able to place emotional action and reaction into their overall value proposition. I have been fortunate to work with one of those companies in the financial advisory and wealth management space. This particular organization not only places a high value on the Experience for the client but is also introducing a cognitive approach to its actual deliverable. This company believes that the science of understanding how people react emotionally and how they feel about money should be combined with the art of providing specialized advice. It is very possible to include emotion in the value deliverable, and there are only a few companies that are changing their respective industries by doing so.

While Disney's theme parks have emotion trickling through their every turn of the value proposition, it can be a bit tougher for pure service-oriented or retail companies to interweave emotion into the value proposition itself. And other companies are proving that this can be done and, more importantly, replicated at a very high level.

Four Cognitive Drivers

There are four emotion-driven chemicals released by the human brain that can bring about action through an Experience: endorphins, dopamine, serotonin, and oxytocin. Endorphins provide physical drive and endurance, while dopamine helps us achieve our goals and makes sure we get things done. Serotonin gives us pride and self-confidence, and oxytocin is the chemical behind love and acts of kindness.

To figure out what drives people to actions—like consumption and repeat consumption—we can look at these four chemicals in relation to their reaction to an Experience.

1. **Driving the Experience toward the release of *endorphins* is created by excitement and the thrill of the hunt.** Disney does this by creating anticipation throughout its parks and their presentations— and even while you stand in line. Many of the attractions at Disney have videos and sneak previews of the ride or attraction and have recently even added interactive gaming to the queues, building anticipation of the fun you are about to have.

2. **Driving the Experience toward the release of *dopamine* is created by generating a feeling of accomplishment and pride through specific results.** Some visitors experience this feeling of accomplishment simply by making it to one of their destinations. The immediate impressions upon entrance are overwhelmingly positive. Disney also makes a habit of special rewards like Club 33 for Disney VIPs, the Vacation Clubs, and the myriad of other opportunities to feel as if you have earned something extraordinary.

3. **Driving the Experience toward the release of *serotonin* is created by special recognition and approval.** Disney does this by making everyone feel like a guest and as if he or she was important—and by making the guests feel as if they are part of the show, for example, by going as far as to include them in a performance or by taking action photos of them during the Experience.

4. **Driving the Experience toward the release of *oxytocin* is created by fostering a sense of love and belonging, community, and communication in the employee and customer base.** Disney does this by creating such a memorable Experience that people feel compelled to become Ambassadors just to share and compare their Experience with others'. Disney is not just a destination; it's a community. Just look at all the Mickey Mouse ear hats when you leave one of the parks and on the plane ride to and from the specific Disney destination.

This example of my first visit to Disney with my four-year-old son is a particularly great depiction of all four of the cognitive drivers. We reached the Magic Kingdom, arriving under the train station with Town Square Theater to the right. It's kind of home base for Mickey, where the guests have the opportunity to go backstage and meet Mickey in person. Now here is the science, in four steps:

1. Endorphins are released as you grow with anticipation of meeting one of the most famous characters in the world. The setting, the cast members, and every aspect of this attraction has your heart racing as you get closer to the backstage door.

2. Dopamine is released as you enter the backstage door and are treated as if you are one of the few people in the world who are being given this opportunity to meet the great Mickey Mouse. While this may sound silly to an adult, children often feel as though they have been selected to meet royalty.

3. Serotonin is released as you reach Mickey's dressing room and he turns and says, "Ah, you made it," as if Mickey was waiting for your arrival. Mickey even knew my son's name. Magic! Mickey's new robotic mouth can enable him to carry on a conversation with every person he meets. Mickey asks about your day and gives everyone a hug and a photo.

4. The oxytocin is running rampant at this point as you have such a sense of love and belonging. You exit the building through a perfectly placed gift shop to capitalize on the emotion and then back out into the Town Center, where there are hundreds of guests reflecting and conversing on the amazing Experience they just had.

And that's how it's done! Disney is not alone in its mastery of the cerebral Impression. From the strategy of external storefront displays of hard-to-find products to build interest and anticipation at Tractor Supply to the inspired tradition at Southwest Airlines of clapping in celebration upon reaching the desired destination, the great companies have learned how to create the cognitive Experience. The four cognitive drivers are extremely important and should always be top of mind when strategically forming, executing, or even repairing the overall Experience for your customers.

Quotient Question
How clear is the commitment, and do you have a plan to build emotional Impressions for the customer?

Actionables
The often forgotten sixth sense is the emotion that we create that instills a sense of desire and confidence in the organization, product, or service.

Try this
☞ When first meeting customers, read their face and body language. Temper and hone your comments or presentation skills to match the mood they are in. This will enable you to connect with them and ascertain their attitude so you can learn how to best serve them.

(continued)

(Continued)

Try this

☞ Deconstruct your value proposition and find the opportunities to create Impressions by concentrating on specific emotional attributes within the deliverable that forge a stronger relationship with the client and consumer.

Try this

☞ Focus on building interest, excitement, and anticipation of what could be for the consumer. Find ways to draw in customers and ways to engage them emotionally from the very beginning of the encounter. Build the anticipation of the "aha" moment!

Impression 1.5:
Presentation

Our work is the presentation of our abilities.

—Edward Gibbon

How well you present yourself and your company is clearly an essential component to your success—and the secret to the presentation and the successful delivery thereof is in the planning and preparation process. We know by now, of course, that success doesn't just happen; you must carefully and methodically plan it. Despite the old adage that "practice makes perfect," we have found that practice *doesn't* make perfect; it simply makes a habit. The appropriate statement is "practice makes consistency." At Disney, it is called "rehearsing the show"—in other words, preparing your part to be excellent on a consistent basis.

Presentation boils down to believability. Any bank teller or receptionist job can be monotonous and boring; or it can be positive and enjoyable if you consider yourself a professional who is a cast member of an Exceptional Experience. The same holds true for any job or role at Disney. There are numerous jobs (roles) that require the exact same skills as you would find in a fast-food restaurant worker, a housekeeper, a gardener, a parking attendant, security guard, and multiple others. It is all about the presentation or the show. Every facet of the Experience must be "show ready," or the Exceptional Experience is unattainable.

When you are having a bad day, are sick, or are stressed out, you have two choices: go home or take care of business. Disney calls it "putting on your show face," and you must give it your best because "the show must go on."

Customers do not really care that you partied all night, that you're sick, that you're burned out, or that you hate your job. They aren't being insensitive; but when it costs about $1,500 per day for a family of four and they've saved for a year to visit the Disney theme parks, they are looking for happy, cheerful, positive employees who are bent on ensuring that their family has a great time.

Rehearsing

One of the key components of the presentation that is lacking is the preparation or the rehearsal. The military call them exercises and "war games." At Disney, it is called "rehearsing the show." It's more than training; it is preparing the staff to be ready and prepared for *any situation* that may arise. Preshow prep is all about asking: "Are we ready? Do we have everything we need?"

One of Bruce's responsibilities at Disney World was working with cast members who made live presentations to guests. Bruce taught the cast to use their tone of voice to convey the right message with personality and professionalism. He was surprised at how many cast members had no idea that their voices affected their presentations. The advice that Bruce routinely offered: "You need to put some energy and enthusiasm in your voice." Speaking in this way communicates confidence—and confidence translates to trust.

Scripting

Customers can usually tell when you are being plastic or faking enthusiasm. You come across as insincere if you're just going through the motions. *We asked a group of 100 guests visiting Disney, "How many* of you feel that the practice of scripting is canned and plastic?" Of the people polled, 90 percent said yes. We then asked them, "What percentage of Disney's spiels do you think are scripted?" Fewer than 10 said that they felt that the interactions were prepared ahead of time. The Disney difference here is training personality into each cast member. Only about 1 in 10 of the people polled felt Disney spiels were scripted, yet, according to Bruce, about 90 percent of them are. There is nothing wrong with scripting *if* you make it your own and personalize it in the process.

It's quite amazing and inspiring when all employees, cast members, and Ambassadors work together to concoct a concert of tactics that delivers an excellent presentation. This action and its level of execution are the very essence of the Experience, and when done right, it's Exceptional and amazing to witness.

> We asked a group of 100 guests visiting Disney, "How many of you feel that the practice of scripting is canned and plastic?" Of the people polled, 90 percent said yes. We then asked them, "What percentage of Disney's spiels do you think are scripted?" Fewer than 10 said that they felt that the interactions were prepared ahead of time.

Quotient Question

Are preparation and scripting part of the strategy that insures the Experience is Exceptional, yet genuine?

Actionables

The presentation each employee provides is a reflection of the preparation and dedication each has made to create the Experience.

(continued)

(Continued)

Try this

☞ Create a greeting that fits your personality, not something that is canned and everyone else uses. Here are some samples, but find your own:

- "Welcome, thank you for stopping in today."
- "Good morning, it's a pleasure to see you."
- "Welcome, is there anything specific I can help you find?"
- "Good afternoon, how can we help you today?"

Try this

☞ Build your own Non-Negotiables, your own standard of excellence. Build it as a company or as an individual, and make sure you share it with everyone for accountability.

Try this

☞ Develop an energy and enthusiasm meter. This can be done within an organization, a department, or just individually. Consistently rate yourself and the team. You can even go as far as to track the metrics of your progress.

Impression 1.6:
Professionalism

If you think professional is expensive, wait until you try amateur!

—Paul Adair

Think back to the time when you were a child and you met the first person whose occupation really impressed you—perhaps an airline pilot, train conductor, policeman, pastor, or politician. Chances are you were completely in awe. From the uniform down to the friendly smile or the tip of a hat, you marveled at the persona that you witnessed. This was an inspiring moment for you; you most likely went back to your mother or father and said, "I want to be him or her one day!" This is exactly the Impression that should be the goal for any internal Ambassador of the Experience—and should be the standard for all of us who work in client- and consumer-facing roles.

Does your professionalism make an Impression? It's that simple, yet it can be incredibly difficult to accomplish. You have a very short time to make a positive imprint of yourself and, consequently, the product, service, or company you represent. Remember: to the customer, *you* are the company. If you were the only person customers met during their visit to a store, their opinion of the business might well be determined by their opinion of you. If it is a negative one, they will walk away with a poor Impression of your company as well.

Virtually every business has a desire to make a positive Impression on each of its customers. Yet, what qualities are essential for employees and the company to convey? Trust? Honesty? Positivity? Probably the one quality that best expresses these and more is that of professionalism. When employees and businesses communicate that they are professionals, it is akin to letting customers know "I've got this." There is a level of competence, confidence, and trust that naturally goes with being a professional. That is why training and rehearsing the show is so critical to the success of any company. The more accomplished and competent employees are, the more confident, knowledgeable, and skilled they will present themselves.

Looking the Part

In order to be a professional, you must first and foremost look the part. You absolutely must act the part and be the part—but without looking the part, the rest of the efforts at professionalism could be rendered moot.

According to a recent CNN study, 55 percent of well-dressed employees in the financial sector are more likely to get promoted than others. That's internal. How about an external statistic? Well, in our independent study of financial advisory clients, we determined that customers are twice as likely to do business with someone who is dressed professionally than someone who is not.

Let's start with the individual. We applied our Experience Quotient test to several grocery stores, focusing specifically on two supermarkets in our research. One of them allowed employees to wear jeans in any condition the employee felt like wearing, whereas the other had a dress code that was casual yet professional. Even though a number of employees did not like wearing nice clothes, it sent a subtle message to us that "we are professionals and we thought enough of you to look the part." The other supermarket—not so much.

Looking the part is going to vary from industry to industry, but the level of importance of how professional you look with regard to the industry standard should not vary. This level of intentional professionalism will not only help you with your customers and clients but could also help you as an employee. Take the financial industry as an example. *According to a recent CNN study, 55 percent of well-dressed employees in the financial sector are more likely to get promoted than others. That's internal. How about an external statistic? Well, in our independent study of financial advisory clients, we determined that customers are twice as likely to do business with someone who is dressed professionally than someone who is not.* It makes a difference.

Acting the Part

Looking the part is pivotal—but as we like to say, "the magic must be magic." That means you have to act the part as well, which is simply the art form of being ready. It's amazing how much trust and validity you can gain in a new relationship merely by being prepared, being accommodating, and acting as if you can handle any situation. Acting the part of a professional makes customers comfortable and confident in your ability to deliver. Being a professional makes customers comfortable to make purchases.

Identification

Let's talk about name tags. If you were a Disney employee and did *not* wear your name tag, you wouldn't be allowed to work that day. Your name tag is the best way to identify you to the guest. Bruce often works in hospitals and notices how many employees do not wear name tags. Name tags are not necessarily needed in all lines and levels of the Experience; in fact, they could be a detriment in the wrong environment. But a certain level of identification of who is the internal Ambassador of the Experience is incredibly important.

Disney now adds the city where the employee was born to the bottom of the name tag. It was a stroke of genius, as it serves as an instant connector and a conversation starter with a total stranger. We've met numerous Disney cast members from Europe, Asia, Australia, Africa, and many of the states. It's easy to forget that the ultimate goal of the Experience is to create relationships and subsequently Ambassadors who will share their Experiences with others. We must make sure that this one main concept of relational Experiences never gets lost in the potential chaos of arranging the concert of tactics it takes to concoct the Experience itself.

The Code

Disney has a very strict dress code. When Bruce was employed there, hair length was monitored. Shoes had to be polished and all cast members were required to wear a costume (uniform) that was specifically designed for the area they were to work in. Uniform or not, all client-service-facing companies must have a dress code in order to create the image and Impression the company desires to convey to its customers. Without it, company employees send mixed signals to their customers of who they are and what they stand for.

If you are old enough to remember IBM in the early days, you might recall that every salesperson and manager was required to wear a navy blue suit with a white shirt and black shoes. Every IBMer looked like a clone and you could spot them a mile away. As rigid as it may sound, it sent a message to their customers: we are professionals and we represent excellence and consistency. That factor alone gave customers a sense of confidence and peace of mind in IBM. It matched the brand and its ethos. You can't put a price tag on that.

Quotient Question

From appearances to greetings, is professionalism paramount and executed when addressing the customer base?

Actionables

Being a professional is to deliver excellence in every aspect of your job and to not be willing to accept anything less than excellence.

Try this

☞ Create and, more important, adhere to a dress code that epitomizes the level of professionalism that you seek to portray. Make sure your attire and code match the spirit of the clientele and the expectations of the customer. Make all forms of hygiene a priority. The idea is to not be overbearing with rules but to take pride as individuals and as a team as a reflection of the professional brand.

Try this

☞ Take note. Create a visual and mental image of the attributes of the best person who has ever performed a specific role or position. Take note of the person's mindset, as well as how he or she dresses, approaches customers, deals with hostile people, recovers from a service disaster, and so on. Identify these unique qualities and then design an action plan for how you can apply those skills to your performance.

Try this

☞ Develop a self-talk—one that brings your mindset up to that of your skill set. You have heard this before and it may seem like a cliché, but it works: if you think the part, you will act the part! It is important for you to present yourself as confident and knowledgeable. Your level of confidence creates in turn a sense of confidence and trust that the customer places in you.

Impression 1.7:
Pristine

I will not let anyone walk through my head with their dirty feet.
—Mahatma Gandhi

In the late 1940s, Walt Disney would always save Saturday as "Daddy's day" with his two girls. Walt's favorite place to take them was to the local amusement park and let them play for hours while he would watch them and dream. Walt was never impressed with the caliber of the employees who worked at amusement parks and carnivals at that time, and was disgusted with the shoddy maintenance and the low standards of cleanliness he observed. He would often say to himself that if he were to ever build an amusement park, he would do it differently. It would be clean, the workers would be pleasant and nicely dressed, and it would be a place where people could feel safe and that the whole family could enjoy together.

The experiences from Daddy's day became the seed of an idea that ultimately would change the face of amusement parks—and the world—forever. While on a train trip, Walt decided to design his own park, but one that would be very different from the parks he was accustomed to. It wouldn't be just about rides or a midway or carnival barkers; it would be made up of different themes and even different eras of time. He wouldn't even call it an amusement park because of the negative connotation. No, this would be a *theme* park. In that moment, he created an entirely new industry—and a new Experience was born.

In *Walt Disney: An American Original* (Disney Editions, 1994), author Bob Thomas writes that Walt visited county fairs, state fairs, circuses, carnivals, and national parks while researching the idea of Disneyland. He studied the attractions and what made them appealing, and whether people seemed entertained or felt cheated. Apparently, his most depressing experience was seeing Coney Island—he found it to be battered and old, and the ride operators seemed to be hostile.

Then Walt had the chance to visit Tivoli Gardens in Copenhagen, which has been operating since 1843. Walt was apparently very impressed with how spotless and clean the park was—full of bright colors everywhere and even priced within most families' budgets. It was filled with fun music, great food, and many of the friendliest and most courteous employees he had ever encountered. That was the spark and model that Walt had been searching for, as he thought to himself, "Now *this* is what an amusement park should be!"

He vowed that Disneyland would be spotlessly clean from the very beginning. And cleanliness became one of the pillars of Disneyland. A journalist who toured Disneyland shortly after it opened predicted, "The Park will never stay clean." But Walt insisted that it would, because "people are going to be embarrassed to throw anything on the ground." Walt was a big believer in the fact that customers react accordingly to their surroundings.

What Is Pristine?

Both Bruce and I have worked and consulted in numerous organizations and industries. Whether hotels, banks, airlines, grocery stores, restaurants, or law firms, one expectation remains constant: cleanliness. *In a survey Bruce recently conducted, over 65 percent of women stated that the first thing they check when they walk into their hotel room is the condition*

In a survey Bruce recently conducted, over 65 percent of women stated that the first thing they check when they walk into their hotel room is the condition of the bathroom. If it isn't clean, they'll complain or even move on to another hotel.

of the bathroom. If it isn't clean, they'll complain or even move on to another hotel. Most people have the same expectations of hospitals. If the bathrooms aren't clean (public or private), they immediately associate it with the quality and even safety of the medical facility.

Our thought was to title this section "cleanliness," but our objective goes beyond just "clean." Cleanliness is often taken for granted in many businesses. Image and Impression need to be deliberate, planned actions, not an afterthought. *Pristine* takes cleanliness to the next level. You will see this statement several times throughout this book: people don't want average anything; they want excellence.

Pristine Is Everyone's Job

It's astounding to think that Disney World manages to maintain 28,000 acres spotlessly, yet your local convenience store, church, or car dealership sometimes can't keep the litter off its tiny parking lot. Disney accomplishes this by making it every cast member's responsibility to pick up trash whenever they see it. That's the only way Disney can keep the sprawling property tidy. One day Bruce was walking down Main Street in the Magic Kingdom. Someone had discarded a cup across the street, about 20 feet to his right. As he passed the area, a manager stopped and said, "You passed right by that cup. Why didn't you pick it up?" Bruce said, "I'm sorry, but I didn't see it." The manager responded, "It's your responsibility to see what others can't or won't." From that point on, Bruce was always on the lookout for anything that appeared as an inhibitor to the Experience.

Very few people actually enjoy cleaning, which isn't really a surprise. After all, who honestly likes to drain sinks, mop the floor, take out trash, dust, and clean bathrooms? But these things are everyone's job. Regardless of who you are, no matter what your title is, maintaining cleanliness and looking pristine is the job of every person who works in your company. As we've learned from Disney, if you don't do it, who will? And when we fail to do it, we all suffer as a result.

When Michael Eisner was still CEO of Disney, someone asked him what his number one job was and he said, "To pick up trash." That's quite a statement from a guy who was making $50,000,000 per year! A clean, spotless, visually pleasing environment is everyone's responsibility, no matter what your title is.

The Difference

I recently toured a Tractor Supply store in Thompson Station, Tennessee, and former CEO Joe Scarlett pointed out how clean the parking lot behind the store was. That's right, behind the store. Joe remarked, "If you want to see how committed the employees are to maintaining a clean environment, check around back!" You see, the commitment to the pristine standard is above and beyond clean. Pristine is not merely making sure the areas the consumer sees are tidy.

During the day at a Disney park, the custodial division's primary job is to pick up trash and take care of anything that detracts from the Disney show. But the real heavy-duty cleaning takes place after hours. During the third shift—midnight to 8:00 a.m.—they bring in industrial power hoses and literally hose off every street, sidewalk, and area that guests encounter. Everything gets thoroughly cleaned *every night*.

There are so many things involved with an Experience that we cannot control. We simply must master the ones we can. Pristine is not just clean; it's above that. It's the attempt at perfection. Whether you are running a taco stand or a chain of 50 five-star hotels, pristine is one of the Disney inspired Non-Negotiables and differentiators of the Exceptional Experience.

Quotient Question

Are the outside and the inside of the facility in pristine shape, and are the appearance expectations of your people clearly outlined and respected?

Actionables

Cleanliness or lack thereof often creates either a positive or a negative impression that both customers and employees have of your organization.

Try this

☞ If there is a cleanliness issue, have a policy of empowerment. Take ownership and resolve it, ASAP! It is imperative that you take cleanliness personally. Do not call a janitor, and do not wait for someone else. You are not above any job—*you* do it. A lack of cleanliness reflects poorly on everyone, especially the brand of the organization.

Try this

☞ The first thing in the morning, every morning, take a walk around the outside perimeter of your building(s). Take a bag and pick up cigarette butts, aluminum cans, coffee cups, newspapers, napkins, and anything else that will detract from who and what you are as an organization. If there is no building, engage the same process within your department, office, or work area.

Try this

☞ Make it a point to see that there is a rotating duty every two hours for each department to be responsible for observing the cleanliness of their area and even the bathrooms. It shouldn't be assigned to one department or to one person within the department. A good schedule would be 11:00 a.m., 1:00 p.m., and 3:00 p.m. every day your business is open to the public.

Impression 1.8:
Pride

Disciplining yourself to do what you know is right and important, although difficult, is the high road to pride, self-esteem, and personal satisfaction.

—Margaret Thatcher

Of the top 25 theme parks in the world, Disney owns the top 8 spots and 9 of the top 10. Nearly 35 years since its opening on October 1, 1971, the Magic Kingdom still attracts 18,000,000 visitors each year. How—and why?

The reason the Disney parks have been so successful is also the primary reason *your* people and *your* company can succeed or fail. We believe this essential ingredient—one that's often missing in many of our people—is *pride*: pride in who we are, where we came from, and especially pride in our product, our service, and our purpose.

There is a reason why Disney has been able to survive for 60 years at the top of the theme park food chain: there is a certain level of pride in everything they do. Employees who don't add pride to their work are merely going through the motions and pretending to care. Far too many times, the "this is just a job" mentality shows through in personal apathy—an attitude that dooms us to mediocrity. *According to Shaw & Ivens, 85 percent of business leaders agree that*

> *According to Shaw & Ivens, 85 percent of business leaders agree that traditional differentiators alone are no longer a sustainable business strategy.*

traditional differentiators alone are no longer a sustainable business strategy. Organizations need something more to differentiate themselves, and having internal pride and employees who wave your flag as Ambassadors is a perfect way to start.

I was in a Ritz-Carlton Hotel in Fort Lauderdale, Florida, recently and ordered a root beer. The problem was that there was no root beer to be found on the premises. This was no issue for the gentleman behind the bar; he simply went down to the local drugstore and bought a six-pack of A&W. When he returned, I asked about the incredible service at Ritz-Carlton and why it appeared that he took a great deal of pride in his role. The gentleman replied, "It is the empowerment over the unsaid expectation." What an answer—and what an Experience!

Pride in the Company

When employees take pride in the company they work for, it shows in a variety of ways. These are the internal Ambassadors that we speak of throughout this book. They are often far more loyal and dedicated to their organization's success. It shows in the extra effort they demonstrate. They are the first to brag about their company and their service deliverable. If you do not have internal Ambassadors, you can forget about developing customers and clients into external Ambassadors who will share their Experience with others. Every company is searching for employees who are dedicated, have a strong work ethic, and are committed to being excellent. If employees truly care about the success of the company, they will naturally care about your clients' or customers' well-being.

Honey Bucket

One of Bruce's favorite stories about Disney pride happened during the daily 3:00 parade on Main Street. A newspaper reporter brought his family down to Disney World for a vacation, and was watching the parade near the castle hub. As the 30-minute parade was nearing its end, he witnessed something he had never seen before. The Calliope (a colorful six-ton pipe organ on wheels) was being pulled by six Percheron horses (a Percheron looks like a quarter horse, but is the same size as the Clydesdale horses that pull the Budweiser wagon) that weigh 2,000 pounds each.

Trailing behind the Calliope was a young man from the custodial department pushing the Honey Bucket. Let us tactfully describe a Honey Bucket: it is green, three feet tall, and 18 inches in diameter, on wheels. It is used to store the "deposits" that the Percheron horses sometimes leave on the parade route.

The young custodian looked like he was having the time of his life, as he would wave at the crowd, smile, laugh, and joke with guests. He seemed to be having a ball. He made it look like *he* was the star of the show. The reporter was so captivated by the attitude of the young man that he told his family, "Wait here—I'll be back in a few minutes." He then proceeded to follow the young man with the Honey Bucket through the parade route to the gate in Frontierland. Just before the young man exited the parade, the reporter stopped him and asked him a question: "I can't help noticing that you seem to be having the time of your life, yet you are shoveling horse manure. How do you do that?"

The young man replied, "Well, sir, I'm fairly new in the custodial division and I was assigned to work the Honey Bucket detail during the parades. My manager said that if I did a good job on the Honey Bucket, I would only have to work it for a month but if I didn't, I would be stuck here for six months. So, I decided to be proud of my work and become the best Honey Bucket person who had ever worked at Disney World!"

Taking Pride in Your Work

The work you do is a reflection of the pride that you take in giving your best. Those individuals who display a poor work ethic and have no pride in their work are often satisfied with substandard efforts and mediocrity.

Regardless of the job you do, taking pride in it and doing your best will make all the difference in the world. Personal pride is a great motivator. It represents the who, what, and why we do the things we do. In our years training, we often tell the participants, "If you aren't proud of what you do and where you work, get out—because you are stealing from yourself and your future, and, most important, you are stealing from the company." Just like a master artist proudly signs each of his or her paintings, we too reflect the level of pride that we present in our work. Remember, those individuals who are bent on delivering their best often have very few regrets, as they leave a trail of success everywhere they go. Oh—and they never get stuck on Honey Bucket detail for long.

Quotient Question

Does each employee demonstrate a sense of personal pride in his or her service and in the organization?

Actionables

Pride is the essence of why we do things and the engine that drives us to be our best and not merely focus only on ourselves.

Try this

☞ Ask yourself, "Who am I doing this for?" The work you do is for the customer, but the reason you are doing it is often greater: for your spouse, your children, your parents, or others you genuinely care about. It is for *you!* Sometimes desire has a greater purpose than today.

(*continued*)

(Continued)

Try this

☞ Make a decision every day: "Today, I will give my very best at everything I do." This is a form of encouragement and exhortation that should be done in the mirror or with a coworker. If and when you can no longer do this, then talk about it with someone or it may simply be time to find something else to do.

Try this

☞ Imagine that you are a world-renowned painter or sculptor. The very last thing that goes on every masterpiece is your signature. Visualize your signature on each interaction your have with a customer. Bring the same level of excellence to each task you do, as it is a direct reflection of the pride you have in yourself and your work. Ask yourself, "Would I sign this?"

Impression 1.9:
Likeability

I've trained myself to illuminate the things in my personality that are likeable.

—Will Smith

We have discovered two attributes in our research that top virtually every list of what customers want, need, and expect:

1. Were the employees friendly?
2. Did they make me feel welcome and important?

The level of the Experience would be improved dramatically if organizations could just manage those two concepts. Yet not many companies do a consistently excellent job at either of those two basic components. Disney does, but not just because it's a fun place; it's because the people work hard to *make it fun*. The key in all of this is simply to be likeable.

Like a magnet, likeable employees and Ambassadors of the Experience tend to draw others to them. Customers like to be around them, and coworkers enjoy working with them. Though it might sound simple, likeability skills involve much more than smiling and giving good eye contact. They include complimenting, affirming, encouraging, and displaying kindness, courtesy, and respect.

Some employees are not "people" people. They dislike working with customers and seem to resent the very idea of helping them. These employees tend to repel customers and coworkers. You can fake it for only so long before the real you will come through. A business owner would be wise to place such employees in arenas that do not require dealing with customers.

Friendly people come across as competent, confident, and interested. They seem to like their jobs and customers. Some employees gripe, "We're professional! We don't need to be friendly." That's arrogance! Competence and knowledge are important, of course, but imagine if every one of your coworkers was friendly and worked at getting along with each other. Wouldn't it improve morale, teamwork, respect, cooperation, and customer satisfaction and make work more enjoyable? Likeability among coworkers usually trickles down to the client. The customer can literally feel an atmosphere of likeability.

The Platinum Rule

We've all heard our entire lives how important it is to apply the Golden Rule. But what does that really mean? By definition, the Golden Rule simply means to treat others in the same manner in which you would like to be treated. However, we actually believe the Golden Rule is incorrectly understood. Other people don't necessarily want to be treated just like you would want to be treated, because your likes and dislikes might be far different from theirs.

To us, the Golden Rule means, "Find out what others like and want and then treat them accordingly." We prefer to call this the Platinum Rule because it gets to the heart of the Golden Rule's meaning. The principle of the Platinum Rule is to treat others in the way that they would most like to be treated and not as *you* might like to be treated. This will always involve treating each person with respect, kindness, and value, which will allow you to unlock whatever precious metal in the relationship you are looking for.

The "I Like You" Principle

Several years ago Bruce was working in a hospital and the chief nursing officer (CNO) asked to talk with him. She said, "Let me tell you a story that just happened to us. The other day, I met with one of my nurses, Cathy, in my office. I said, 'Cathy, as you make your rounds today, I'd like for you to do something for me. Before you walk into a patient's room, I want you to say to yourself, 'I like you.' As you are working with the patient, say to yourself, 'I like you,' and as you finish with that patient, say, 'I like you.' Cathy said, 'That's silly. Why?' I said, 'Just do it!'"

Several hours later, Cathy ran into her CNO and said, "You set me up!" The CNO said, "No, I didn't." Then Cathy said, "Then why was everyone so nice to me today?" The CNO said, "Cathy, you're a good nurse; but you aren't consistent. You tend to let the petty trivialities affect your day. You're often like a yo-yo. When you don't get to work with a certain shift, you're upset; when you don't get the patient you wanted, it affects your day; or when you don't get to go on break when you wanted to, it ruins your mood, and the patients and your coworkers have no idea what kind of mood you're in."

She continued, "But today you exerted an effort to 'like' each of your patients *before* you entered their room and, unbeknownst to you, you projected that you liked them and they reciprocated and liked you back." Stunned, Cathy asked, "Would it work like that all the time?" The CNO responded, "I'll bet it would."

Try it yourself. Before you are about to deal with an angry customer or a difficult coworker, say to yourself, "I like you," and see if it doesn't begin to improve your relationships with others.

Friendly Returns

In most cases in life, you receive exactly what you give to others. Zig Ziglar put it this way: "You can have everything you want and need if

you will just help enough other people get what they want and need."
Your company, your department, and your organization will be as nice,
caring, and friendly as you make it—nothing more and nothing less.
And since you can't change other people, *your* work and *your* attitude
are not about others; they are about you. If you're not happy with the
way things are at work, change them. If your team isn't getting along,
address the issue and do whatever is
necessary to work together. Life is like
a mirror; you get what you give. *According
to TARP Worldwide, 68 percent of all
customer turnover is directly due to poor
treatment.* Just be nice, for it cures a lot
of ills.

> *According to TARP Worldwide, 68 percent of all customer turnover is directly due to poor treatment.*

Likeability is often the number one ingredient that customers are
looking for. That's it. Being likeable isn't rocket science; but it is the
science of how you treat people, how much you care, and how well you
get along with others. The Disney model of being friendly, courteous,
and considerate and making people feel welcome has worked for
60 years. The bottom line: nice works.

Quotient Question

How well does each employee demonstrate the qualities of
being friendly; expressing interest; being courteous, caring, and
helpful; and just being likeable?

Actionables

The key to great service lies in each employee's ability to master
the qualities of likeability: to be friendly, kind, courteous, and
caring.

(*continued*)

(Continued)

Try this

☞ Make it your goal to execute F.A.C.E. Impressions:

F. ~ Friendliness: Be kind, personable, considerate, helpful, and caring.

A. ~ Attitude: Always maintain a positive attitude and outlook.

C. ~ Connection: Look for ways to build rapport and a relationship.

E. ~ Excellence: Always strive to deliver excellence in everything you do.

Try this

☞ On a daily basis, use the common courtesies of "please," "thank you," "you're welcome," "my pleasure," and even "my apologies." These phrases are essential to developing likeability.

Try this

☞ Rather than focusing on why others are wrong or misinformed, concentrate on their point of view and directly on their need. Isolate that need and have a steadfast desire to win the moment by turning the tide of the Impression. These decisions to cooperate are game changers within the Experience.

Impression 1.10:
Consistency

Across professions, consistency is a direct product of work ethic.

—Harsha Bhogle

The last element of Impression is to create a level of consistency. One of the primary differences between being an amateur and being a professional is that professionals have developed a high degree of consistency. Most professionals not only are very good at what they do, but also are able to take that level and perform it on a consistent basis. You achieve a certain level of expertise when you're able to combine excellence with consistency.

Why Consistency?

Consistency creates stability for all involved. Knowing what is expected of employees removes uncertainty and any ambiguity. When employees do not know what is expected of them or experience revolving leadership without consistent policies, chaos ensues—and employees become more prone to do their own thing or leave.

Consistency creates a strong positive reputation. When the public and employees know what to expect, word gets out to the outside world. Most people appreciate predictability and do not like surprises—at least when it comes to where they're spending their hard-earned money. And then an interesting feature enters the mix: pride ensues within the employees and they actually *want* to tell others where they work.

Everyone knows what is expected. In computing, it's called WYSIWYG—"what you see is what you get." Consumers experience a sense of confidence and comfort in knowing what they will receive on a regular basis. Loyal customers are incredibly valuable. *The White House Office of Consumer Affairs tells us that loyal customers are worth up to 10 times more than their original purchase.* Loyalty is created through consistency and simply cannot be ignored.

> *The White House Office of Consumer Affairs tells us that loyal customers are worth up to 10 times more than their original purchase.*

The Deliverable

In a service-oriented or customer-facing organization, the deliverable—that is, the actual service or product offering—is mission critical. This is where the value proposition has its opportunity to shine. It is the opportunity to connect the offering with an Experience. It is also the easiest way to convert Ambassadors from your client base who are committed to sharing their Exceptional Experience with others.

The deliverable at Disney is the show. It encompasses everything from the anticipation to the hotels, the parking, the entrance, the service, the food, the visuals, the characters, the attractions, and the fun. It is a "happiness destination" that's executed to perfection every day.

In order to create optimum movement in the world of consumer referrals, the deliverable must be consistent and repeatable. It does you or your organization no good to be able to create the magic only once or for every third or fourth customer. You must be able to replicate that magic/deliverable/Experience time and time again, leaving lasting Impressions that burn the Experience into the minds of your clients and future Ambassadors.

Quotient Question

Are the Impression models and the skills you employ consistent throughout the Experience, and are they scalable and repeatable?

Actionables

All progression in any endeavor is a matter of consistency of excellence, beyond the price your competition is willing to pay.

Try this

☞ Commit that you will be consistent in every phase of your deliverable. Then determine what you can repeatedly execute with consistency. You must build consistency as your foundation before you can instill excellence in execution.

Try this

☞ Create a model and a tangible manual of excellence that you can copy and deliver each and every time. Train the skills and examine the outcomes of the execution tactics so that they can be further developed and repeated as part of the culture.

Try this

☞ Prepare a commitment manifesto for the organization. For the Experience to be consistent, the whole is the sum of its parts and the Exceptional can never be reached or repeated without everyone committing to consistency in the deliverable. There is no price tag you can place on dependability.

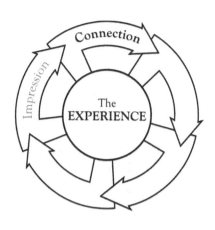

Chapter Five
Principle 2: Connection

Pay special attention to those who, by the accidents of time, or place or circumstances, are brought into closer connection with you.

—St. Augustine

There are few companies that have been able to master the art of connecting personally with their customers. One of them, of course, is Disney. Another good example is Southwest Airlines, which operates according to the brilliant supposition that you can actually create a loving environment and even make your customers laugh during one of the more unpleasant marketplace consumptions—commercial air travel. I was recently on a flight where one of the attendants had changed the lyrics to the great Willie Nelson song "On the Road Again" to "In the Air Again." The song was funny and inventive, and it made me forget for a while that I was on a plane.

Relationships are the epicenter for all meaningful and long-term product or service associations. The beginning of the relational inflection path or the catalyst of the process of building a new relationship is the connection between two individuals, which is essential to creating the experience.

Every customer wants to feel important, and to be met by friendly staff members who make him or her feel welcome. If your company doesn't make that its top priority, it has already failed at delivering one of the basic components and foundational principles of service.

The Connection is a pivot point between contact and the relationship. Converting clients and customers from consumers to Ambassadors hinges on your ability to create the cerebral, emotional, and personal Connection. An Ambassador is so sold on your people, product, and service that he or she becomes a walking advertisement for your company. Ambassadors can be a gold mine for your company because they don't cost anything and they pay enormous dividends. However, the cost of *not* having them could be significant.

Value Is the Linchpin

Connection builds rapport and a relationship, however brief, with the customer. Deeper than mere communication, it is how we build the trust, confidence, and loyalty by laying the foundation for a long-term relationship. The secret behind communication and building relationships can be found in the accretive nature of the Experience, or, for lack of a better word, the value.

It is the same with people who have an initial Connection and the beginnings of a relationship. Unless the initial spark in a relationship comes from "love at first sight," the pivot point of most relationships derives from a transactional relationship in which each party derives value from the other. And even love at first sight doesn't always last if there isn't something deeper and more binding at work.

Value goes beyond mere utility as well. Of course there is value in getting a cup of water from someone when you are thirsty. But the

Experience goes much deeper than just a cup of water with a smile. Emphasis on this must be top of mind for everyone in the organization. *Defaqto Research claims that 55 percent of customers would pay more for better service.* The connection must begin with something extraordinary—more than ordinary, and more than utility. Relationships and revenue are on the line.

> *Defaqto Research claims that 55 percent of customers would pay more for better service.*

The Role and Rules of Value

Value should always be real (helpful), relevant (impactful), and timely (useful). There should also be a degree of showmanship in every client interaction. The value must be accompanied by the Exceptional and the relational touch. This is truly what sets companies like Disney and Southwest apart. Showmanship does not imply that something is fake. The excitement, the enjoyment, and the Connection with the customer are not only real; they are delivered on a level that stands apart from other client/employee engagements. Ponder this thought for a minute before moving forward and reading about the Ten Disney-Inspired Non-Negotiables. You now can begin to understand why the folks at Disney call it a "show."

Connection: Ten Disney-Inspired Non-Negotiables

Connection 2.1: **Communication**
   The foundation of the Connection and understanding that everything you do communicates.

(continued)

(*Continued*)

Connection 2.2: **Deliberate**

A commitment that no customer is left out! Everyone must receive the full Experience.

Connection 2.3: **Personalize**

While Experiences must have consistency and be repeatable (science), employees must also master the art of making customers feel as though every interaction has been custom created for them.

Connection 2.4: **Affirmation**

This involves making clients or consumers aware of how important they are.

Connection 2.5: **Knowledge**

This is the ability to truly know every aspect of the product, process, or service offering, as well as everything possible about the client and customer.

Connection 2.6: **Interaction**

Mastering the points of interaction: face, phone, and tech based (e-mail and social).

Connection 2.7: **Respect**

This is common courtesy and the art of putting others first.

Connection 2.8: **Trust**

Finding ways to build trust with those who have limited contact with you.

Connection 2.9: **Relationship**

The inflection points to establishing relationships and lifelong customers.

Connection 2.10: **Finishing**

Finishing the job and seeing the Experience all the way through to the end.

Connection 2.1:
Communication

Communication, the human connection, is the key to personal and career success.

—Paul J. Meyer

The foundation of all service and the mortar for all relationships is communication. Everything you do communicates on some level; you cannot avoid it. Literally everything you say or do tells the consumer and others a great deal. It's not just the words you say, your tone of voice, eye contact, facial expression, and body language, but also your personal and corporate presentation down to the last detail that all represent you and your company.

> *In his landmark book Silent Messages (Wadsworth, 1971), Dr. Albert Mehrabian categorizes communication into three parts: 7 percent words, 38 percent vocal tone, and 55 percent body language.*

In his landmark book Silent Messages (Wadsworth, 1971), Dr. Albert Mehrabian categorizes communication into three parts: 7 percent words, 38 percent vocal tone, and 55 percent body language. Even though the words are important, it is difficult to derive actual meaning from the words alone. The primary communication inhibitor is perception on the part of the hearer. Words often have multiple meanings and can easily be misinterpreted without the other two components: tone of voice and body language.

Tone simply implies all of the components that make up speech: inflection, speed, pitch, personality, clarity, volume, and energy are just some of the elements that make up a person's voice. We've all heard this expression: "It's not *what* you say that is important, but *how* you say it." Words by themselves are often neutral, but it is the addition of emphasis and inflection that clarifies their meaning.

The third and most defining component of communication is body language. Body language includes things like posture and how you stand, eye contact, gestures, facial expressions, and the mouth. As another expression goes, "Your actions speak so loudly that I can't hear what you say." If there is any question about meaning or congruency, it is body language that lends the most weight to its definition.

We don't have the luxury of seeing body language over the phone yet, but we will in the next few years. The breakdown on a telephone call is that 14 percent of communication is the words and 86 percent is the tone of voice, which clearly highlights the fact that the tone of your voice is much more important over the phone than it even is in person.

Congruent and Consistent

The key to communication is congruence. Do your words, your tone of voice, and your body language all match? If not, you have lost believability. For instance, someone can use the most eloquent words with the most enthusiastic, positive tone of voice—but if he or she refuses to give you eye contact or looks bored to tears, you wouldn't believe anything that person has to say.

Remember: the customer's perception is all that counts. The customer's perception is *your* reality. So, when you work with a customer, you don't start from your point of view or even from the reality of the situation; begin instead with what the customer believes reality is. Your customer may be 180 degrees off base—but you always begin where he or she is and start from his or her point of reference.

While part of the Disney cast, Bruce coined the phrase "*guest perception*" that is still being used in the consulting world today. Here is how it works: you invite a friend or someone from another business who has never been at your company to evaluate your business as a new "guest." You explain that you would like that person's "perception" of how your business comes across to a total stranger. Ask if he or she would be willing to come and observe your people, your building, your products, the attitudes of your staff, your professionalism, and the service process from his or her point of view. That information can be invaluable and tremendously beneficial to your current and future business. It's like having a focus group of one.

What Does "Good" Communication Look Like?

Good communication happens when everyone is on the same page and heading in the same direction. It is clear and involves clearly understood behaviors and expectations. Good communication is always designed, and good communicators never panic or become exasperated. While deliberate, good communication also remains very fluid. Good communicators look and sound professional and execute at a high level of consistency, leaving customers with a feeling that they are truly valued at all levels. Good communication comes from practice—as practice makes expertise apparent, and clients feel valued inside the Experience.

Quotient Question

Is there emphasis on and execution of the quality, form, and frequency of communication when interacting with the customer?

Actionables

You cannot *not* communicate. Everything you do tells your customer and your coworkers how much you do or don't care about serving them.

(*continued*)

(*Continued*)

Try this

☞ Create a sense of congruency; make certain your words, actions, attitudes, and tone of voice match. Otherwise your message is confusing and meaningless. Try taping yourself, and think about turning this into a monthly exercise or training technique.

Try this

☞ Rehearse what you will say to your clients and customers. Make certain you connect with the customers on their level. Use terminology that is simple, clear, and easily understood. Prepare and then perfect the script through repetition.

Try this

☞ Put a smile in your voice each time you answer or talk on the phone. It will inject personality into your voice and make you sound more interested in callers and interesting to them. Give authority to your coworkers (especially those seated near you in the organization or call center) to comment when your communication quality wanes. No one hears you more than they do!

Connection 2.2:
Deliberate

All our dreams can come true if we have the courage to pursue them!

—Walt Disney

Disney is not only the largest theme park company in the world, but it is also one of the best—which doesn't happen by accident. Walt Disney World is the largest single-site employer in the United States. With nearly 70,000 cast members, you don't create that consistency without being specific and intentional in your service. Disney has built-in structured systems that are designed to deliver consistent levels of excellence in each of the 1,500 different job classifications.

Disney has done all of this by mastering the art of Connection within every facet of its operation. The result has been the ability to build an endearing image and reputation for the young and young at heart all over the globe.

Being intentional and deliberate is the launchpad to building a relationship. Again, most of what we describe in this book as the Experience deals first with the Experience that you are committed to causing for others.

Terminology

Walt Disney was very much a film and movie aficionado. That was his heritage and passion. So it stands to reason that when Walt envisioned

Disneyland, he would borrow many of the concepts, principles, and terminology that he was so familiar with. His model works. Each of the Disney parks and many other theme park companies still use the concepts and terminology today.

For the purposes of *The Experience*, we want to provide you with the Disney mindset of how intent is used to guide the entire Experience. Disney has gone so far as to create its own vocabulary and terminology that drive its entire operation. In the list of some of the nomenclature, you'll recognize a few terms from prior chapters.

Disney Nomenclature

Guest: Every customer and visitor who comes to a Disney park.

Cast member: Any employee who works for a Disney park.

Audition: Interviewing for a job in the park.

Role: The position the employee was cast into.

Traditions: Disney orientation.

Onstage: In the presence of a guest.

Backstage: Not in the presence of a guest.

Costume: The uniform designed for the respective position the employee is working.

Show: Any onstage (in the presence of a guest) presentation.

Good show/bad show: How well or how poorly the presentation was done.

Onstage versus Backstage

One of the most important concepts to come from the theater and the movie industry is that of being onstage or offstage. *Onstage* simply denotes how a person is to act and behave whenever he or she is within view or earshot of the guests. Anytime you are around customers, you must give your best; be courteous, helpful, friendly, and outgoing. When any employee is onstage, he or she must be "on" and delivering 100 percent, since the show must go on regardless of how you feel.

Backstage includes the times when you are away from the guests, such as on a break, in the stockroom, and in any other nonguest area. This is where employees can relax, let down their guard, and not have to be "on" with the customers. Backstage is also the place where the planning, training, and coaching happen. Whether it's a musical performer or a server at one of the restaurants, nothing at Disney makes it onstage until it is ready to be executed with precision.

Good Show versus Bad Show

The terms *good show* and *bad show* are extensions of the onstage/offstage concept. A good show is anything that fits into the context of service excellence or the Disney show. If behaviors, actions, or attitudes are a natural part of the service and fit the motif, Disney calls them "good show," or the behaviors that are considered appropriate to be onstage.

The contrary is also true; that is, any attitude or negative behavior that violates the show or distracts from the message is considered "bad show," or behavior that should be offstage. For example, a cast member in a Space Mountain costume would never walk through Adventureland and Jungle Cruise or Pirates of the Caribbean, because it would violate the scene and destroy the illusion. Anything that does not add to or complement the show is unacceptable.

How does this apply outside of the walls at Disney? You would not want to be in a serious and confidential discussion with a client in a law office or discussing important investment decisions as a financial adviser when the door of the conference room is flung open by office colleagues who failed to check the conference room ledger. Or imagine being in a waiting room at a hospital where two of the nurses are discussing how crazy their kids are within earshot of a patient. This speaks volumes to the patients, and tells them that they are not important even though it is not direct communication with them. "Bad show!"

The proverbial bad show simply cannot be allowed. This is the focal point of being deliberate. You can control only so much within the customer Experience. According to Ruby Newell-Legner, it takes 12 positive Experiences to make up for one negative one. Control what you can, and limit or eliminate the occurrence of bad shows.

In order to avoid the crisscrossing of Disney cast members through an area that would violate the Disney show, an extensive network of tunnels called the Utilidor was built into Disney World at the very beginning. It is somewhat similar to a hexagon with numerous outlets to each of the locations. This allows cast members to enter into their areas without violating the show. The problem was solved at Epcot by creating an outside perimeter around World Showcase and Future World that would allow cast members to be dropped off at their exact locations. It's clear that Disney has gone to great lengths to maintain the onstage show for each of its guests. It is intentional, deliberate, and quite often flawless.

Quotient Question

Do employees make a deliberate attempt to put on a good show and build a relationship with the consumer?

(*continued*)

(Continued)

Actionables

Being intentional and deliberate is the launchpad to building and then protecting relationships.

Try this

☞ Experiment with using the term *guest* or another preferential word to refer to your customers. Also think about referring to your problem clients and customers with terms of endearment as well. It will change the way you view customers and especially how you treat them.

Try this

☞ Place a sign in the break room or offices denoting that these locations are "backstage." This will remind everyone that when they depart the confines of these organizational safe zones, they are going back "onstage"!

Try this

☞ Break each customer experience into individual components. See that each part (each role) is done with excellence and consistency. Think of the show as a concert of tactics that come together for the total Experience.

Connection 2.3:
Personalize

I miss the personalization that Vegas was. Everyone knew everyone by their first name.

—Wayne Newton

While Experiences must have consistency and be repeatable, an Exceptional Experience has the rare trait of making every interaction feel like it was customized specifically for each and every consumer. The ultimate goal of the Connection Principle is to establish a certain rapport with customers by personalizing the product or service rendered to best fit their specific needs. Companies who have perfected the science of discovering what customers want, need, and expect are better prepared to pull off what many would call impossible. Take Google as an example of a company that provides an Internet service based on expectations and needs. Its Experience and even its acquisition model are built around serving clients' needs at the personal level. Google often buys companies to add to its customer services portfolio long before its current customers even know that they need the service. The effort to anticipate and learn the desires of the potential and current client base is what places many companies ahead of their competition. Our goal is to take all services to a deeper level by challenging you to personalize what you say and do.

Demographics versus Psychographics

Demographics are statistical data: height, weight, age, occupation, race, gender, or a snapshot of who that person is at that point in time. Demographics provide information for and are relevant only today, but tell us nothing about the future.

A far better tool to help us is to ascertain psychographic information, which is attitudinal in nature: wants, desires, interests, goals, likes, and dislikes. Whereas demographics tell us about the present, psychographic information tells us where you want to go and what we need to do in order to prepare the Experience.

Disney posts individuals from the marketing department on a daily basis to do just that. Their role is to find out what visitors did and didn't like about their time at a Disney park, but to also learn what they would like future rides, attractions, shows, and Disney parks to look like. It is important to see how we're doing today, but even more critical to figure out where the customer desires for us to be in the future. And we can ascertain both of these through psychographic information.

When Epcot opened in 1982, much of what we projected the future of the world would be was built of brushed stainless steel and Plexiglas. Shortly after Bruce created his position to improve service for Disney in 1983, he sent a memo to leadership about a specific ride at the Land Pavilion, stating, "We need to project Epcot as connecting people to a bright future. It is essential that we provide the personal touch and make our people the star of the show."

He was referring to a 10-minute ride in the Land Pavilion called the Land Boat Ride. It is a labor-intensive ride that takes guests through the four seasons of spring, summer, autumn, and winter to show how fruits and vegetables will be grown with and without soil. Disney had been spending about $800,000 per year just on labor for that one ride. Management found that if the ride were automated and had no cast members, it would become substantially more cost-efficient.

However, Bruce's memo had an impact on the executives, especially the part where he claimed, "We are losing the personal touch that Disney is renowned for." As a result, they kept the ride operators. Management also made a commitment to train with greater emphasis on empowering each ride operator to personalize the performance by adding personality and life to the presentation. That is what gives any presentation that believable and personalized feel: you must inject yourself and the personal touch to everything you do.

First-Name Basis

Your name is the most important thing you own, which is why every cast member at Disney is required to wear a name tag at all times. Every name tag has the cast member's first name imprinted in bold letters, and every cast member is required to be on a first-name basis with others. Disney has discovered that the use of titles—Mr., Mrs., Ms., Miss, Dr.—often creates invisible walls or barriers between you and the other person. While it felt awkward at first to call former Disney CEO Michael Eisner "Michael," it works. First names don't detract from one's professionalism, and they do help connect you with others more quickly.

At Tractor Supply stores, the employees are encouraged to learn one customer's name per week. Imagine walking into a retail or department store and one of the employees greets you with the best sound in the world: your own name! These are the subtle yet gigantic differences between the Average and the Exceptional Experiences.

When patients go through the admissions process at the Mayo Clinic, they are asked the routine questions: insurance, history, address, and demographic information; but then they are asked some non-intrusive questions, such as favorite color, anniversary, kids' names and birthdays, favorite vacation, pets, where they were born, and so on.

On the second page of a chart outside the patient's room are all the questions and answers. Every employee—nurse, lab technician, dietitian, or housekeeper—is required to look on the chart and ask one question related to the responses. Patient satisfaction in that hospital is unprecedented. People want you to talk to them about things that interest them. That's how you connect, and it is a very important aspect of the Experience and the show.

Connections create loyalty, and loyalty can be the foundation to creating Ambassadors. One of the best ways to show a client or customer you care is to personalize his or her Experience. *According to* Leading on the Edge of Chaos *by Emmett Murphy and Mark Murphy (Prentice Hall, 2002), a 2 percent increase in customer retention has the same effect as decreasing costs by 10 percent.* People deserve better than what they are receiving in the marketplace today. Connect with your consumers and benefit your organization by making the customer part of the show. Commit to personalizing their Experience.

> *According to* Leading on the Edge of Chaos *by Emmett Murphy and Mark Murphy (Prentice Hall, 2002), a 2 percent increase in customer retention has the same effect as decreasing costs by 10 percent.*

Quotient Question

Do the employees of the organization make an effort to learn customers' names and other specific information about them in order to customize and personalize their interaction and Experience?

Actionables

While Experiences must have consistency and be repeatable, we must also master the art of making every interaction feel like it was custom created for the individual.

(continued)

(Continued)

Try this

☞ On a regular basis, seek feedback, verbally and through survey questions, to ensure you are meeting and exceeding your customers' expectations. Ask loyal customers to provide you with specific things that they would like to see happen that would increase the level of their Experience. Document those things and make them happen.

Try this

☞ Make it a weekly habit to learn and use a customer's name. Our name is the most personal thing we own, and it is reassuring when someone calls us by it. Also, use your first name. Using your first name helps you connect with the customer more readily than using titles before your name.

Try this

☞ Identify three specific actions you can do that will make your customers feel like they are VIPs. Think about randomly selecting customers for your highest level of Experience. It's not an upgrade; it's a way to show that anyone and everyone is important.

Connection 2.4:
Affirmation

To give someone a blessing is the most positive affirmation we can offer.

—Henri Nouwen

One of the most effective ways to build a relationship with others is to consistently affirm them—to highlight their good qualities and minimize the less than positive ones. While affirming strangers might sound peculiar, therein lies the secret: they're not strangers at all. Rather, they are guests in your Experience—and if you can make them feel like family, you are on your way to converting them into Ambassadors.

When Bruce was a performer at Disneyland, his group was sent to Japan to promote Disney and to encourage the Japanese citizens to visit the United States. In fact, the name of the show was "Come to America." They toured 14 cities over 37 days, performing the show in a new city about every other day. During that time, Bruce was privileged to meet and work with a number of Japanese people and got the chance to experience their customs, lifestyle, culture, food, and values.

One of the terms he learned from the Japanese was *saving face*. As he was told, it was their custom *not* to insult or offend anyone, even if they were wrong, in front of another person. Their philosophy was: "I will say whatever I need to say and do whatever I need to do to make you look good in the eyes of others."

What a great philosophy. How can we affirm other people, make them feel good, and even make them look good in the eyes of their peers, colleagues, friends, and family? Can you imagine what a difference you would create in the overall Experience if this tactic was utilized internally and externally? We would greatly enhance the lines of Connection.

Affirm through Acknowledgment

Here's an interesting question: what is the biggest insult you can give to another person? Answer: to ignore them. If I call you a name or insult your intelligence, I am still treating you as a person. However, if I totally ignore you, I am treating you as an object or a nonentity. And we do this every day. There are some very simple ways in which we can counteract ignoring others. We can start by expressing interest, which demonstrates that you care about them.

Here's another interesting question from a study we conducted: what is the opposite of love? If you answered hate, you would be in the company of 80 percent of the people we polled; but you wouldn't be correct. In fact, many of the attributes, qualities, and intensities you find in love you will also find in hate. So, love and hate are actually somewhat parallel emotions but with different displays of interaction. The opposite of love is actually indifference. Only 5 percent of people got it right in our study, but 89 percent agreed when we presented it to them in this fashion.

If I am indifferent toward you, you mean nothing to me. Indifference has

Here's another interesting question from a study we conducted: what is the opposite of love? If you answered hate, you would be in the company of 80 percent of the people we polled; but you wouldn't be correct. In fact, many of the attributes, qualities, and intensities you find in love you will also find in hate. So, love and hate are actually somewhat parallel emotions but with different displays of interaction. The opposite of love is actually indifference. Only 5 percent of people got it right in our study, but 89 percent agreed when we presented it to them in this fashion.

some very close cousins—apathy, ambivalence, and complacence are just as offensive. There's really no greater insult to customers than to ignore them.

M.M.F.I. Principle

Everyone you know is wearing a sign around his or her neck. Some people's signs are very small, some are normal size, and others are enormous. Each sign is invisible, but they all have four letters on them: M.M.F.I. Every day people are displaying their signs in a variety of actions, behaviors, and words, they are telling you M.M.F.I. or Make Me Feel Important. They are saying, "What are you doing to make me feel special, valued, and needed?"

Every person wants to feel important because everyone *is* important. Every employee and every leader in your organization must apply the M.M.F.I. Principle and let others know how important it is for them to have a great Experience and how critical they are to the success of your business.

Quotient Question

How well and how often do you compliment your customers or clients and make them aware of how important they are?

Actionables

It is imperative to make your clients or customers know how important they truly are.

Try this

☞ Ask for your clients' and customers' opinions, ideas, and input. Look for ways to compliment them every chance you

(continued)

(*Continued*)

have; sincerely compliment their attire, their taste, their demeanor, and their interests. Practice this; it will help you at home, not just in the marketplace.

Try this

☞ Intensely listen to your clients and customers, giving them your undivided attention. This action shows them that you care about them and about meeting their needs. If any customer has requested information or a product, follow up to ensure you have taken care of their request. That demonstrates importance.

Try this

☞ Come up with a list of positive affirmations for your customers. Also, try reinforcing the clients' choices and decisions when you agree, but offer suggestions in a tactful manner when you don't. Disagreeing with their selection or choice can also mean you care. You are the expert!

Connection 2.5:
Knowledge

Knowledge is power. Information is liberating. Education is the premise of progress, in every society, in every family.

—Kofi Annan

The more you know your customers, the more effectively you can take care of their needs. Knowledge is essential in order to learn about and understand your customers. If you fail to spend time getting to know your customers' likes and dislikes, then you can't help them. Service is not merely about selling something; its goal is to meet people's needs. If you don't care about what your customers need, then you don't really care about them.

There are myriad reasons why customers purchase goods and services: to fulfill a need, to feel good, to meet basic necessities, or for convenience, price, value, name recognition, compulsion, fear, protection, replacement—the list goes on. Regardless of the reason, we can categorize most purchases into one of two areas: emotional and logical. Emotional purchases are often the "I want" response, or compulsive feelings. That is why grocery and department stores places profitable items like gum, candy, doughnuts, and magazines next to the cash register—to appeal to people's attention and compel them to grab something at the last minute.

Emotional purchases frequently end in buyer's remorse. Far too many times a skilled salesperson talks someone into purchasing a product or service because of how the salesperson makes the customer feel, only to have the customer regret making that purchase mere days or even hours later.

Logical purchases are often referred to as "I need" or justified purchases. These have been generally well thought out and occur when the customer has a framework of knowledge in order to make a well-informed purchase. Our responsibility is to provide objective tools and guidance in order to help customers acquire the knowledge to make a logical versus an emotional decision.

Knowing Your Client

It can be a challenge to try reading people. As we discussed earlier, people will often tell you how they feel and how you can help them without even speaking a word. The first step in your Connection process should be one that involves reading the client and then determining how to use that knowledge. The more you know about any given subject, the better prepared you are mentally to improve.

No one can presume to know what someone else wants unless one develops a deep understanding of the other person's needs and desires. And we cannot uncover this kind of information merely by reading faces, gauging tone of voice, or noticing body language. We gain this sort of expertise via research and the study of people's social styles. *A recent Forrester study shows that 68 percent of companies are using Voice of the Customer (VoC) programs for feedback.* Don't get left behind by your competition. If you are going to be an expert on something, be an expert on those who pay your salary—your clients.

> *A recent Forrester study shows that 68 percent of companies are using Voice of the Customer (VoC) programs for feedback.*

Know Your Product

Products come in all forms; they can be virtual, tangible, or even a complete deliverable. As you're doubtlessly aware by now, Disney's product is the Happiness Experience. No matter what kind of product you have, you must know anything and everything about it. Have you ever had salespeople who knew very little about what they were selling? How professionally did they come across? We have to be the experts on our products and value propositions. There is no shortcut to the event or the sale.

Quotient Question

Are the employees trained to be experts on their customers as well as on the service, product, and Experience deliverable of the organization?

Actionables

If knowledge is power, then the desire to learn is the prerequisite to all growth and achievement.

Try this

☞ Pride yourself on knowing more about each of the products and services you provide than anyone else in your organization. Develop three descriptive points for each product or three differentiating aspects of the organization's value proposition. Then seek to learn how to best support these points with feature and benefit statements (what the points mean to the customer or client) that you can readily share with the consumer.

Try this

☞ Create personalized notes or utilize technology and customer relationship management (CRM) systems for your regular customers and special items they always look for.

Try this

☞ Learn the name of one customer's spouse, child, grandchild, pet, and so on per week. There are numerous exercises to

(continued)

(*Continued*)

help you remember names through associations and faces. Use them to learn the names, and you will be one step closer to creating Ambassadors for your organization. It's impressive to know someone's name. It's the knowledge of the ones they care about that can help move the Experience from Great to Exceptional.

Connection 2.6:
Interaction

Each contact with a human being is so rare, so precious, one should preserve it.

—Anaïs Nin

Take a look at each of the various interactions a customer may have while engaging one of your products or services. How many different points of contact does the customer encounter? One of the secrets of mastering the Connection is to master the points of interaction: face-to-face, telephone, e-mail, and social media.

In his book *Moments of Truth* (Ballinger, 1987), former SAS Airlines CEO Jan Carlzen calls them "moments of truth." He defines a moment of truth as "anytime anyone comes in contact with any person within SAS Airlines and forms an opinion." Carlzen found that the average customer has a total of five interactions with SAS employees, and the airline has 10 million passengers per year.

He goes on to explain, "We don't need to focus on the 50 million moments of truth; we just need to improve the five interactions." Carlzen was right. In one year with the entire airline industry in the red, SAS Airlines went from losing $8 million one year to making $92 million.

In every business, there are as few as four or five things that if improved and fine-tuned would dramatically change your business and the perception the world has of it. Your objective is to identify those golden four or five things. We are presenting five (the I. C.A.R.E. Principles) to you here in the book.

Every customer who does business with you has very few contacts or interactions with your employees. If you can effectively manage and ensure that those interactions are successful, you will change your model and your customers' perception of you. *The White House Office of Consumer Affairs states that it is seven times more expensive to acquire a new customer than it is to retain a current one.* It is very important to make sure that the organization as a whole understands why this is such an important facet of the Experience.

> *The White House Office of Consumer Affairs states that it is seven times more expensive to acquire a new customer than it is to retain a current one.*

Disney employees realize that each point of contact presents a great opportunity to deliver either Disney magic or mediocrity. They pride themselves on trying to be excellent with every guest encounter. For instance, the Disney cast members who have the most direct interaction with guests are the custodial employees—the people who sweep the sidewalks, pick up trash, and clean up spills. They are the reason Disney is so clean and why guests rarely find trash anywhere on property. Although their primary responsibility is to pick up all of the trash no matter where it may be, their other responsibility—of equal importance—is to answer questions, give directions, and help guests have a positive experience.

Master the Contact Points

Regardless of what your specific responsibility is, everyone is expected to become an expert in the points of contact, such as face-to-face, phone, and technology-based interactions. No one is expected to be an expert on day one; but most employees should have a handle on this within three to six months.

When you call Walt Disney World and ask any question, the closing response is "Have a magical day." For many businesses, how you answer the telephone is often the customer's first point of contact. If you (and your company) lack personality, professionalism, and enthusiasm in your voice as you answer the phone, then you're missing a great opportunity to connect with a future customer.

The next contact point is often in person. Face-to-face interaction sets the tone for how the customer sees both you and your company—and, as previously discussed, your customers evaluate you in a very short amount of time. If you are not putting your best foot forward, then you have lost an important connection point.

It is becoming increasingly imperative that you have a serious presence within social media through blogs, Facebook, Pinterest, Vine, Twitter, and LinkedIn. Ten years ago, virtually no one received their primary information about your company through social links, but today it is a prerequisite to do business in a high-tech world.

Again, we have so very few opportunities to have that moment of truth or magical interaction with a guest or customer that we have to make them count. Our customers today have an opportunity to affect our brand positively or negatively. We must manage those few points of contact effectively and ensure that each of them is part of the Exceptional Experience we and they are after.

Quotient Question

Is there a commitment to and then clear execution of a relational Experience with in-person, phone, and technology-based communication?

Actionables

Building relationships and connections is both tactical and methodical. You must master and have protocols for all of

(*continued*)

(*Continued*)

the points of customer interaction—face, phone, and tech-based (e-mail and social).

Try this

☞ Break down each encounter or moment of truth within a typical service cycle, evaluate them, and explore one or two ways that each interaction can be improved. These moments are the inflection points in relational momentum.

Try this

☞ Whenever possible, invest in small talk with customers in order to build rapport, which helps them relax and creates a sense of trust. Get them talking about themselves: where they were born, favorite hobbies, kids or grandkids, music—anything that will help you connect with them.

Try this

☞ Once a month, meet with the service and support team to discuss any points of contention or congestion in the service cycle. If you are on the service and support team, meet with sales and other departments to share feedback and collaborative ideas. Create an action plan to enable everyone to create a seamless and positive Experience for the customer.

Connection 2.7:
Respect

There is no respect for others without humility in one's self.

—Henri Frederic Amiel

One of the most important aspects of Connecting lies in the level of respect you give to other people. Respect lays the foundation for how we do business, and serves as the basis for civility. It is how we show consideration for others and demonstrates the fundamentals of caring, politeness, and being a genuinely nice and thoughtful person.

Disney has always had four standards of service that have remained constant since the opening of Disneyland in 1955. Dick Nunis and Van France created these, which are still the core of everything Disney does. The four original standards were Safety, Show, Courtesy, and Capacity. In recent years, they have been modified slightly to reflect a fresh emphasis on Disney values:

1. **Safety:** Staff members take every precaution to ensure that each guest is safe.

2. **Courtesy:** Our goal is to treat each guest as a welcomed VIP.

3. **Show:** Every aspect of the Disney show and cast member must be excellent.

4. **Efficiency:** The entire guest experience must be smooth and seem effortless.

Of the four, safety and courtesy are first and foremost as they deal directly with respect for the guest and customer. Without these, the show is worthless and efficiencies will not matter in the least.

The Role of Safety

In any business, safety must come before anything else. When Bruce was a supervisor in the Magic Kingdom, a guest was watching the Main Street Electrical Parade in a gazebo at the castle hub one night. In order to get a better view of the parade, she stood on the back of a park bench and held on to the decorative vines made of ornate ironwork under the gazebo roof. During the parade, she slipped and caught her wedding ring on the iron vine, and it broke her finger. Even though the cast members were not able to alleviate her pain, she was very touched at the extraordinary level of effort that the Disney cast and medical team exerted in order to comfort her.

Here was a disaster that would ruin any vacation, yet the guest went out of her way to thank everyone for the tremendous efforts made to assist her. Safety and the relational component of the mental ownership of someone's well-being in any organization must be paramount.

The Role of Courtesy

One of the primary hallmarks for Disney employees is that they must demonstrate the basic tenets of every Disney cast member. First, they must be a friendly and courteous person. The foundation of respect begins with common courtesies. Yet the common courtesies that many of us grew up learning are no longer common.

The foundation of respect and common courtesies is humility. In order to forge a relationship and a Connection with a customer, you must first have the heart and mind of a servant. Without a certain measure of humility, you simply cannot fake it.

Respect, humility, and the common courtesies are essential to the Experience that your organization is creating. *According to Forrester, a 5 percent increase in customer retention can increase profits up to*

According to Forrester, a 5 percent increase in customer retention can increase profits up to 125 percent.

125 percent. Respect is a catalyst for loyalty and is a foundational precept at Walt Disney World; it should be in your company as well.

Quotient Question

Is the client relationship of utmost importance, and do you always make customers feel as though they are respected and are always right?

Actionables

The art of putting others first is an important ingredient within the Experience. It is a foundational pillar and the entrée to any successful relational exchange.

Try this

☞ Set your own personal standards each day to improve your attitude and your interaction with customers, and to create consistently excellent service. Try establishing standards that are even higher than the organization's.

Try this

☞ Anticipate and correct problems. Look for trip hazards, spills, visual impairments, and even verbal compliance traps that could result in a safety issue for your customers or coworkers. Correct problems as soon as you are aware of them.

Try this

☞ Make a list of the common courtesies. Perhaps even laminate them and place them in your pocket. Strive to become an expert in Courtesy 101. Listen, give your full attention, and say "please," "thank you," and "you're welcome."

Connection 2.8:
Trust

Building trust requires talking and thinking about trust.

—Robert Solomon

Webster's dictionary defines trust as the "assured reliance on the character, ability, strength, or truth of someone or something." The foundation of trust is character, something we don't hear very much of with any degree of consistency today.

Trust is the basis of all strong and, more important, *ongoing* relationships. In fact, when you misuse or lose the trust of customers, you often lose their patronage for good. We have surveyed both employees and customers for the purpose of this book as to the most important attributes they expect from a boss and from the company they are doing business with, and trust is almost always one of the top three prerequisites.

ABCs of Trust

To the customer, the ABCs of trust are the price of doing business:

A ~ Accuracy: Are you up front and transparent in everything you do? This includes pricing, negotiating, and delivering all information, however critical or trivial.

B ~ Believability: Do you deliver integrity and honesty to everyone? This includes truth in the labeling or branding of your service offering, value proposition, and products.

C ~ Congruency: Does everything you say and everything you do align? This builds a sense of consistency and dependability that makes people want to return.

Why Is Trust So Critical?

Trust is critical because consumers and customers want you to be authentic. There is enough lying going on that the American consumer is already wary of most things advertisements tell them. If customers and clients cannot count on you to be consistent, ethical, and trustworthy, then you have no foundation in your relationship.

We can think of the customer/provider relationship as a marriage. As a provider, you want the customer to stay with you for life. While the features and benefits are different in this type of arrangement, the relational path is similar. Customers have a sense of when they feel others are being plastic and fake. Many can read when we are disingenuous and are suspicious when they feel they are being misled or lied to. Whether it is truly happening or not, perception is reality and you will never salvage the relationship if the trust is lost.

Your organization cannot afford for this to happen. When trust is lost, people talk about it. As we have discussed, people who share negative Experiences far outnumber those who share positive ones. *According to a survey conducted by Dimensional Research, 86 percent of buying decisions were influenced by negative online reviews.* Trust is tough to build but very easy to tear down, and it will affect your organization one way or another.

According to a survey conducted by Dimensional Research, 86 percent of buying decisions were influenced by negative online reviews.

Trust in Connecting

Always keep in mind that we are building relational Experiences and external Ambassadors of our organizations. Do not forget the little BIG things. Start by simply keeping your word. Few things destroy a sense of trust as when we fail to keep a promise. It wasn't too long ago that major contracts were agreed upon by a handshake and a simple comment, "My word is my bond." That is where integrity lies, within the individual's ability to keep a promise regardless of circumstances. We have all heard the advice to "underpromise and overperform"— because it is true.

Keep communication simple. The more ambiguous and nondescript the information, the greater the degree of distrust. Often the most effective style of communication is to be clear and concise, without the in-depth legalese verbiage. The more confused your customers are, the greater their tendency to doubt you.

Sharpen your listening skills. The biggest problem in communication today is our lack of listening skills. We focus too often on how we are going to respond to others' comments so that we fail to listen clearly to the message. Employ active listening skills; this involves summarizing the other person's information and repeating it back in a simple, clear response. This does two things: it ensures that you understand the message, and it lets the other person know that you are both on the same page.

One and Done

Trust is everything. Even though it may take years to build a foundation for a relationship, one incident, one failure, or one lapse in judgment may be all it takes to destroy credibility.

I grew up in the Charlotte, North Carolina, area, near the Christian theme park called Heritage USA built by Jim Bakker. In the mid-1980s, it was the third most visited theme park in the United States, behind Walt Disney World and Disneyland. Mr. Bakker had the world by the tail, but greed through a lack of financial transparency and fraud, followed by a lack of honesty and trust involving an affair, destroyed his entire empire. Remember: in life and in business, you often have one chance. If you blow the one chance you have, you may never get another.

Let's take the reverse side of the story. In Chicago in 1982, someone opened bottles of Tylenol and placed cyanide capsules inside. As a result, Johnson & Johnson recalled all Tylenol from all grocery shelves. Experts predicted the end of Tylenol, but Johnson & Johnson's proactive approach and new tamper-proof packaging reassured its customers that safety (trust) was an important ingredient in Tylenol, and today the company is stronger than ever. Johnson & Johnson lost hundreds of millions of dollars in the recall, but has more than made up for it since. The company executives were told that they did not have to go so far as to remove the entire inventory nationwide; however, they knew it was the right thing to do.

When someone lies or misleads you and you lose the trust factor, it is very difficult if not impossible to regain your credibility. Trust is a difficult thing to rebuild once it is broken.

Quotient Question

Is there a commitment and a clear plan to build trust with every consumer who comes in contact with your organization?

Actionables

Trust is imperative to creating an Exceptional Experience. The true craft involved here is finding ways to do so with limited interaction and contact with the customer.

(continued)

(*Continued*)

Try this

☞ Take a close look at the information provided and the process from each customer interaction. Play devil's advocate with them. Make every interaction honest, with integrity, and clearly stated for their benefit. Believability comes from their being able to know that they can rely on what you are saying and that they can trust that your intentions are pure.

Try this

☞ Be proactive. Tell the customer up front what all of the costs, fees, and charges will be. Any hidden or extra costs create doubt and mistrust. Remember, most customers do not want surprises.

Try this

☞ Write down every promise or declaration made. Be a person of integrity. Keep your commitments or don't make them. Control what you can control by having a system of keeping your word.

Connection 2.9:
Relationship

Adapt yourself to the things in which your lot has been cast and love sincerely the fellow creatures with whom destiny has ordained that you shall live.

—Marcus Aurelius

To whatever degree, all service has the makings of a relationship opportunity. Even those situations where service lasts only a few seconds, like the initial greeting of a customer, the immediate response after a problem arises, or even a compliment at the right time for a client having a bad day, the opportunity still has relational potential. To what extent is another matter. Some services appear to be more tactical in nature (simply fulfilling a service), whereas others are encapsulated as part of the Experience. Some intentional relational connections are part of the service offering, whereas others are scripted as part of the relational Experience deliverable. The difference and the level of Exceptional is up to you.

> More than 70 percent of guests at Disney parks are repeat visitors, many of whom have come multiple times.

More than 70 percent of guests at Disney parks are repeat visitors, many of whom have come multiple times. What is interesting about their frequency is that they have come to call aspects of their visit "my favorite park," "my show," or "my restaurant." It's almost as if they have taken ownership of the park and the pride that goes with it. They have in fact created a bond and a relationship with certain aspects of the park and with those employees who are connected with the park, thereby making them external Ambassadors of the Experience.

That is why relational service—or service that is derived to create the foundation of a relationship—is so important, especially at Disney, when it costs an average family nearly $1,500 per day to visit. They have built a relationship and the trust that goes with it over years and, in some cases, over generations. Disney has guests who have enjoyed a Disney park for nearly 60 years.

Relational Service

From the beginning of the Impression, on through to the points of interaction and all the way to the climax of the Connection, our Principles come together to form a certain imprint on the brain. As we have discussed in this Principle, the desire for our businesses, our organizations, and our service offerings is to first make Ambassadors of our own people, and second to create external Ambassadors of the Experience out of our customers. We want them to share their *positive* Experience with others. Relationships are built on emotional, tactical, or economic Experiences. A bad Experience equals no relationship—and that leads to no Ambassador and no sharing. It's that simple. The slippery slope is that it can take a lifetime to build a relationship and a minute to crush it. With regard to our topic of relational Experiences, you can do everything right to connect with the consumer, and then one mishap, handled poorly, can ruin the relationship forever.

I like the way Joe Scarlett, formerly the head of Tractor Supply, puts it. He says, "Our customers are not a transaction unit; we want a lifetime relationship with them." The secret behind building relationships and creating relational Experiences begins with the way the people you desire to connect with are viewed and valued. Are you looking for dollars or relationships?

The Science of Relationships

While the concept of building relational Experiences is simple, relationships themselves can be quite complex. There is truly a science to building them. In my book *Relationship Momentum* (Dunham Books, 2013), I discuss the need to build Mass in the form of three specific relational equities: Brand Equity, Value Equity, and Ambassador Equity. I often like to present the science of relationships in equation form, and we all know that anything multiplied by zero is, well, zero. The secret and science of relationships is having all three equities if you are interested in propelling a brand, an idea, or an ideal.

Here are the three relational equities in more detail:

1. **Brand Equity:** Who you are and what you stand for. This equity is more about ethos than it is about a logo.

2. **Value Equity:** The magic! Are you truly producing value? Is it real, relevant, and escalating for the consumer?

3. **Ambassador Equity:** Harnessing the power of a strong brand and a true value proposition to convert customers to fans and ultimately to Ambassadors.

For your organization, your relationship currency in the marketplace is simple: create relational Experiences. If you build real relationships, you will be referred and recommended, and that's when an organization begins to see demonstrative growth.

Quotient Question
Does your organization have a commitment to building relationships and developing lifelong customers?

Actionables
Relationships take time and loads of effort, but they are the originating catalyst of loyal Ambassadors who will tell the world of the Experience you create.

(continued)

(Continued)

Try this

☞ Have a system and/or use technology to keep regular customers informed of sales, specials, or opportunities that are of interest to them. Follow up and get back to customers to ensure they are satisfied. They will learn that they can count on you. You also must execute on this to truly build Ambassadors out of your clientele.

Try this

☞ Add value by offering something more than customers expected or giving them an extra. Communicate this value regularly and continue to be dedicated to its evolution. Value is the basis for a relationship. A strong value presence prepares customers to be converted to Ambassadors, and it tells them you value their business and want them to return.

Try this

☞ Have a sign or visible credo that describes your commitment to building relationships and lifetime customers. Also make your commitment to developing Ambassadors (the result of the relationships you create) visible, as you always want to prepare customers for their conversion to promoters of your business and Experience.

Connection 2.10:
Finishing

Courage means to keep working a relationship, to continue to seek solutions to difficult problems, and to stay focused during stressful periods.

—Denis Waitley

It is abundantly clear that there is a lack of follow-up and follow-through within the walls of the service offerings in American companies today, whether it's seeing the Experience through to the end or checking the temperature of the Experience and the burgeoning Connection. The tactic of continuation and the procedure of understanding how the customer is feeling or enjoying the Experience is often lost in the barrage of tactics within the deliverable.

Vehicular Disappointment

When Bruce was younger, he used to buy used cars and sell them. He has purchased 45 cars during his life, so he has some experience with car dealerships. When his kids were in grade school and junior high, his wife felt they needed a bigger vehicle to transport multiple kids to events, games, and other activities. With the help of the local dealership, Bruce ordered a specific type of van from the factory. He had to wait six weeks, but it was worth the wait.

During the entire sales process, he and his family were treated very well. The staff at the dealership bent over backward to answer his calls and take care of his concerns. Everything was great up until he received the vehicle. Then, about six weeks after delivery, he went back to the dealership with a problem—and was treated almost as though he was a con artist. No one seemed to remember him, they forgot his name, and they dismissed him as an inconvenience rather than treating him like a valued customer. To this day, the instant he receives an e-mail from them to "come on back," he deletes it. He said he still likes the specific brand of car, but has since changed his allegiance because he will "never buy from or recommend that dealer again!"

The Genuine Article

Contrast the preceding story to my Experience with Andrews Cadillac in Brentwood, Tennessee. I had never owned a Cadillac before meeting co-owner Nelson Andrews. I was compelled to come in to look around as the Andrews family has supported one of my charitable interests over the years. I was met on the lot immediately by one of the salespersons, who asked if there was anything he could do for me. One thing led to another, and I ended up purchasing my first Cadillac. It was a good car, but I was clearly buying a good car from *great* people. The difference maker for me was the Experience during but even more so after the purchase.

My salesperson was 31-year Cadillac veteran John Bearden. John loves his job, his coworkers, and Cadillac. John has made it his policy to know family members' names, birthdays, and important happenings, and even calls his family of customers several times a year to check on their Experience. I am a repeat buyer from Andrews Cadillac and John, and will be again. In fact, most recently, I was even talked out of purchasing a current-year car for an older one since the body style was the same but it was in impeccable condition, with ultralow mileage. I bought the older one, saved a ton of money, and am happily still driving the same style and look of the car I wanted. From the first Impression to the finishing touches, John, Nelson, and the team at Andrews Cadillac commit to executing. How could I ever purchase from anyone else? That's a great example of finishing the sale, and creating an Exceptional Experience.

Why Follow-Up Is So Critical

Following up and finishing are when the service starts, not before the sale or even during the sale. You demonstrate the real proof of whether and how much you care in the after-the-sale Connection. That is when employees and sales personnel exhibit how much they are genuinely interested in you and your satisfaction.

Ultimately, follow-through is really about building the long-term relationship with your client or customer. If you are interested in more than a one-time experience, then how you follow up and follow through with every customer is vitally important for six reasons:

1. **It demonstrates sincerity.** You genuinely care about the customer.
2. **It shows integrity.** You are a person who keeps your word.
3. **It demonstrates credibility.** You have built a foundation of trust.
4. **It values the relationship.** Service is more important than the sale.
5. **It creates repeat business.** The customer wants to come back again and again.
6. **It creates word of mouth advertising.** The customer wants to tell others about your company.

By practicing these essential values, you turn your customers into willing advertisers for your company, resulting in a tremendous return on investment (ROI). If you remember the remake of the Christmas movie *Miracle on 34th Street*, you will recall the "real" Santa Claus, Kris Kringle, was paid to play the fake Santa for Cole's Department Store in New York City. When a customer complained to Kris that Cole's was out of a specific toy, Kris cheerfully suggested she find it at the competitor and at the sale price. When the customer told this to Kris's manager, he was furious and about to chastise Kris until the customer told the manager; "You tell your Santa Claus that he's made a Cole's shopper out of me. Any store that puts the parent ahead of the almighty buck deserves my business. I'm coming here for everything except bananas and toilet paper!"

Following through means looking out for the best interest of the customer. Again, why is all of this important? The first reason is that people just deserve better. Start with that belief and you are ahead of most. Second, you cannot ignore the statistics of what a customer service Experience means to the success of your organization. *Recently, the Customer Experience Maturity Monitor from the Peppers and Rogers Group stated that 81 percent of companies with strong capabilities and competencies for delivering customer Experience excellence are outperforming their competition.* The numbers do not lie.

> *Recently, the Customer Experience Maturity Monitor from the Peppers and Rogers Group stated that 81 percent of companies with strong capabilities and competencies for delivering customer Experience excellence are outperforming their competition.*

When you put the customer's needs ahead of your own, you will differentiate your business from your competitors. When you treat your customers like they would like to be treated, then those customers will become your biggest fans, and in turn, Ambassadors for your company.

Quotient Question

Do you consistently exert an effort to complete the Experience and to follow through every step of the way to ensure that the customer is fully satisfied?

(*continued*)

(Continued)

Actionables

The entire Experience is for naught if the organization does not close each customer engagement with a capstone of excellence.

Try this

☞ Have a system and a process for following up and ensuring that the problem was solved or the opportunity was realized. Even if you turn over an issue to someone else, you *still own* the issue. Get back with the customer to follow up to ensure that the customer has been satisfied.

Try this

☞ Continue to reinvent your greeting, pitch, or engagement template. If the script remains fresh, it will continue to create a connection with others while keeping you and your coworkers excited about the show.

Try this

☞ Reengage at the end of the sales cycle, as what you may think of as being the end actually is the opportunity for the beginning of a lasting relationship. The Experience is a process, as the last thing customers will remember can be just as important as (or more important than) the first thing. Strive to make their last impression even better than the first, and you will find the customers returning to your organization again and again.

Chapter Six
Principle 3:
Attitude

Weakness of attitude becomes weakness of character.

—Albert Einstein

There are a lot of elements that combine to help make the Disney parks better than virtually all other theme parks in the world—but we believe that first and foremost it is Attitude. If we could identify one thing that separates Disney from every other organization on the planet, it would be the way Disney expresses its ideas, beliefs, and corporate identity.

Attitude is the filter of everything you think, say, and ultimately do. It is the lens through which you see the world and the outward expression of inward feelings. The Experience may begin with first Impressions for the consumer, but for those in charge of the Experience deliverables, the first and all-important ingredient is Attitude.

What Is Attitude?

What is inside your mind and your heart is usually expressed by what you do. Renowned former college football coach Lou Holtz said it this way: "Ability is what you are capable of doing. Motivation determines what you do. Attitude determines how well you do it." You can control who you are and whom you become by controlling the way that you think.

Renowned author Charles Swindoll once said, "The longer I live, the more I realize the impact of attitude on life. Attitude, to me, is more important than facts. It is more important than the past, than education, than money, than circumstances, than failures, than successes, than what other people think, say or do. It is more important than appearance, giftedness or skill. It will make or break a company . . . an individual . . . or a home."

This is why we deliberately placed the principle of Attitude in the middle of our I. C.A.R.E. Principles model, as it is the glue of the entire mindset. Without the right Attitude, there is little reason to spend time on Impressions, Responses, and Exceptionals, as there will certainly be no Connections.

Why Is Attitude Important?

Over the years, there have been numerous studies and test groups to determine the correlation between Attitude and success. *The Dale Carnegie foundation has made an interesting discovery in its research. The researchers have narrowed it down to two primary areas of how people tend to get ahead on the job and in life. The first area is technical skills and knowledge. The second area is people skills and Attitude. In search of a secret to success, here is what they found: 15 percent of successful outcomes are due to technical skills and knowledge while 85 percent of successful outcomes are due to people skills and Attitude.*

However, the question that we are all trying to answer should not be: *how can we be successful?* The question should not even be: *how do we get the job done?* That is, *how do we become successful by doing an amazing job?* You must possess some technical skills and knowledge in order to complete a task, of course; but in the conquest for the relational Experience, the amazing job can be unlocked only by the right Attitude and then by combining that with great people skills. We should all be looking to mold great Attitudes, creating the Ambassador mindset that breathes life into our organizations, our deliverables, and our Experiences.

> *The Dale Carnegie foundation has made an interesting discovery in its research. The researchers have narrowed it down to two primary areas of how people tend to get ahead on the job and in life. The first area is technical skills and knowledge. The second area is people skills and Attitude. In search of a secret to success, here is what they found: 15 percent of successful outcomes are due to technical skills and knowledge while 85 percent of successful outcomes are due to people skills and Attitude.*

The Attitudinal Lens

There was a story of a very difficult sixth-grade classroom in Chicago. Apparently, the students were so disruptive that the school had lost three teachers in the first few weeks of school. So a retired teacher named Mrs. Wilson heard of the school's dilemma and offered to help. Even though she had been an excellent teacher, the principal felt it might be too dangerous for her to teach the class; but since no one else would take on the responsibility, he decided to let her assume the role. The principal was so concerned, he even offered to place a guard in the class, but she declined.

After a rough start, the students settled down and began to cooperate. By the end of the semester, they had grown tremendously, and by the end of the school year, they had improved more than any other class in the entire school system. To show the school admin-istration's deep gratitude, the principal threw a re-retirement party for Mrs. Wilson. During the festivities, he asked what she had done to turn around such a difficult and unruly class. She said, "Actually, I have you to thank for their progress. I thought it was a stroke of genius to give me a list of their names and IQs: Mary—123, Mark—127, Bobbie—132, and my most difficult of all, Jesse—141. These were bright kids; they just needed some love, direction, and someone to challenge them and draw out what was inside of them."

When she finished, the principal said sheepishly, "Mrs. Wilson, those weren't their IQs; those were their locker numbers. I just thought it would be a good idea for you to know where their lockers were in case you had to send them home."

Isn't it remarkable how we see people—ourselves included—in a fresh, new light when we adjust the attitudinal lens? Whether we do so on purpose or it happens by chance, the impossible becomes possible. People tend to increase or decrease in direct relation to the expectations they and others have of them. The heart of service is found in the way you choose to see your customers.

The Set of the Sails

Two large sailing ships pass each other, one going north and the other south. They have no power, except for the wind that fills their sails. How can two ships headed in opposite direction use the same wind to power them? It is the set of the sails that determines the direction of the ships. By altering the setting of the sails, you change the direction of the ship. It is the wind that powers it, but it is the "bent" of the sails that gives it its direction.

The same is true of people and organizations. Life and circum-stances power us, but it is Attitude that provides the "bent"—the direction in which we go. The great part is that *we* control the direction because we control our Attitudes. I love this quote by Ralph Waldo Emerson: "Nothing great was ever accomplished without enthusiasm." All of the great successes in any endeavor were filled with passion and enthusiasm. Consider the "set of your sails" as you review the 10 Attitude-related Disney Non-Negotiables. Is your organization powered by passion and an Attitude of enthusiasm—or by one of mediocrity?

Attitude: Ten Disney-Inspired Non-Negotiables

Attitude 3.1: **Idealism**
Every Experience begins with the belief that people just deserve better.

Attitude 3.2: **Choice**
The decision to be committed to creating an Exceptional Experience.

Attitude 3.3: **Desire**
The relentless resolve and decision to carry out the execution of the Experience.

Attitude 3.4: **Yes**
Creating a culture where "Yes" is the rule instead of the exception.

Attitude 3.5: **Happiness**
It's hard for people to not have a positive Experience in a happy environment.

Attitude 3.6: **Optimism**
The power of positive thinking permeates any environment.

(continued)

(Continued)

Attitude 3.7: **Expectations**

Expecting success and preparing employees and clients to expect the same.

Attitude 3.8: **Persistence**

The drive to continue to improve in all facets of the Experience.

Attitude 3.9: **Ownership**

Creating an atmosphere of responsibility for the Experience.

Attitude 3.10: **Illumination**

The knowledge or understanding of how important your Attitude, service, and the Experience you create is to your people and your customers.

Attitude 3.1:
Idealism

Words without actions are the assassins of idealism.

—Herbert Hoover

We all can be a little delusional with regard to the greatness of our own products, ideas, and services. That's okay; after all, if we do not believe in our own ideas, why should anyone else? The problem arises when delusion in the concept turns into delusion when vetting your own service standards and the Experience.

When it comes to idealism and delivering an Experience, the positive nature of this irrational exuberance in our own ideas and organizations can be useful. We must feel that our service offerings have the opportunity to change an industry, geographical landscape, or even the world. If we do not believe this inherently, the Experience is often lost. It's like goal setting; with no goals or no picture of success or a better mousetrap, we often get complacent, apathetic, or bored, and our Attitudes sour.

The Formula

Here's a simple equation to demonstrate the power of Attitude.

$$\text{Attitude} + \text{Belief} = \text{Conviction}$$

Attitude is ultimately your perception of life. Consider two individuals in the midst of a huge rainstorm without an umbrella: one is furious because her new shoes will be ruined, she's cold, she just came from the beauty parlor, and her hair is a mess. A second person is enduring the same storm, but she has decided to have fun, to enjoy the carefree moment, and to let all of her stresses go. Bad things happen to each of us; the question is: what are you going to do about it?

The second component is belief. From our early childhood, most of us are taught to believe in something that gives us strength and a reason to trust. During a hurricane of events when everything around you is in chaos, beliefs keep you grounded and focused. Beliefs are a set of values or principles that are deeply rooted within you and that give you a foundation, a framework for your future. What you believe in is critical to your direction and your success in life, in relationships, and certainly at work.

Every Experience begins with belief that people deserve an incredible product, service, or process. If there is no ideal of a better way to do it and that you can do it, the Experience you and your consumer are looking for will never be achieved. You must first visualize the possibility of excellence long before you can ever hope to achieve it.

According to a recent American Express Global Customer Service Report, 60 percent of consumers believe businesses have not increased their focus on providing good customer service. Among this group, 26 percent actually think companies are paying less attention to the Experience overall.

According to a recent American Express Global Customer Service Report, 60 percent of consumers believe businesses have not increased their focus on providing good customer service. Among this group, 26 percent actually think companies are paying less attention to the Experience overall. Strong customer service and creating an Exceptional or even Great Experience may be a cliché slogan for many organizations but the execution thereof is not the norm. The ideal that consumers deserve better than what they are receiving is a belief that must be shared throughout the organization for the Exceptional to be implemented.

So, Attitudes plus what you believe equal your conviction. Often it is conviction that drives success. If Attitude is *how* you feel and belief is *what* you feel, then conviction gives you the *why* to carry through with your ideals.

Conviction

During his commencement speech at Princeton University in 2010, Amazon founder Jeff Bezos made the following comment: "Will you wilt under criticism or will you follow your convictions?" Every person who ever strived for greatness was chastised and ridiculed at some point for his or her convictions.

Walt Disney had a dream that no one, including his partner-brother, believed in. Walt wanted to make Disneyland a reality. Reporters mocked Walt; experts told him it would never survive without a Ferris wheel and that it wouldn't last more than a year. He personally had to borrow on everything he owned, including his life insurance, just to get Disneyland off the ground, but that still wasn't enough. Finally he approached ABC about his new concept for a show, and the network lent him $500,000 with loan guarantees of $4.5 million for a 35 percent stake in Disneyland to produce his first weekly broadcast of *Disneyland*. Even the bankers told Walt that it would take 11 years to pay off Disneyland. He paid it off in *one* year.

Conviction is more than dedication and just plain hard work. You must combine it with the belief that you can succeed and then compound it with the ultimate enabler, Attitude. If you can do this, no Experience is impossible.

Quotient Question

Is there a congruent belief in the ideas and ethos of the company as well as the ideal of creating the best possible Experience?

Actionables

Conviction is the one attribute that truly differentiates you from other individuals and companies. You must believe that people are worthy and that you are capable of creating the Exceptional.

Try this

☞ Make a habit of listening to motivational talks and inspirational speakers. Whether they are phone downloads, CDs, or in person, this is helpful to shape the Attitude that each individual and the organization is looking for.

Try this

☞ At least once a month, write the word "Purpose" at the top of a page, and then list the convictions that support your purpose and why you believe them. Next, determine what Attitudes and attributes best support each of these.

Try this

☞ Create a vision statement as an individual or as a team to become the best at some endeavor. Let no one stop you; dwell only on succeeding and the positive aspects of your work and vision, and keep a weekly journal of your successes along the way.

Attitude 3.2:
Choice

Destiny is no matter of chance, it is a matter of choice. It is not a thing to be waited for, it is a thing to be achieved.

—William Jennings Bryan

There is nothing easy about building an Experience. There must be a mutual commitment from everyone in the organization to create the ultimate deliverable. The great thing about life is that you *do* have a choice in what you do, where you go, and how you will get there.

Charles Swindol once said, "The remarkable thing is we have a choice every day regarding the attitude we will embrace for that day. We cannot change our past . . . we cannot change the fact that people will act in a certain way. We cannot change the inevitable. The only thing we can do is play on the one string we have, and that is our attitude. I am convinced that life is 10 percent what happens to me and 90 percent how I react to it. And so it is with you."

Ambition and the American Dream

If you were born in another country and lived in that country your entire life until you were 21 years old and then immigrated to the United States, you would have a 400 percent greater chance of becoming a millionaire than a U.S. citizen who was born stateside. That is a true statement that we uncovered in our research—but *why* is it true? There is a "fire in the belly" of those who have been oppressed for years that Americans simply do not have. There is an innate desire to utilize their talents and skills. There is a work ethic that many will work three jobs just for a chance to live the American dream.

Over the years, numerous people from Nigeria, India, Iran, or Russia have said to us things like "I wish you Americans could live in my country for just one year; you couldn't handle it! You have no idea how good you have it here! Come live in India in a caste system where you have no choice about what you will become, or live in Haiti where the annual income is $200 and there is poverty everywhere. We finally get to America where there are no limits, where we can drive a taxi for three years, then purchase the taxi, and 10 years later we own the company."

It is that choice and that chance for greatness that drives people. Many of us have lost the desire to make a difference in ourselves because we have become complacent. Either we have lost the "fire in our bellies" or it was never there to begin with. As head of an organization, you must find ways to inspire your employees to choose to have the right Attitudes. *Disengaged workers cost the economy $300 billion or more per year, according to InteliSpend research.* How much are the choices of the disengaged costing you?

A Covenant

We rarely talk about the term *covenant* anymore, but it is a great term to incorporate in each of us if we are to succeed. A covenant is simply an ironclad commitment or guarantee that you will do something. In the parlance of our topic, a covenant is a contract with yourself or with others to fulfill a role or a responsibility. The people who truly desire to succeed make a covenant within themselves that they are not going to take the shortcut to greatness. They believe that "Average never inspired anyone." Several years ago, Bruce saw a billboard that caught his imagination. It said: "*Yagottawanna* . . . if you don't wanna, you ain't gonna." It really doesn't matter how smart you are, how good-looking you may be, how talented you are, or how adept you are at whatever you do. Those things help; but if you don't *want to* strongly enough, if you don't have the desire, you cannot be successful at anything.

A business also makes a covenant with its clients—a brand promise that should be a part of the value proposition. Whether or not you are intentional enough to communicate this or convey the covenant to the client, this cerebral contract should align with the core values of the organization and then must be carried out to its fullest extent. Just like every other Principle we discuss in this book, Attitude is a choice, and unless we make the right one, it is impossible to create an Exceptional Experience. It is not enough just to talk about service in a slogan. We have to make the decision to create something Exceptional.

Quotient Question
Has a decision been made to commit to an Exceptional Experience, and do the employees believe in and support that decision?

Actionables
Attitude is a choice, and it is the controlling factor that tempers everything you do.

Try this
☞ Provide yourself and perhaps your coworkers a daily reminder that your Attitude is a choice. It can be a sign like the famed Notre Dame "Play Like a Champion Today" sign that the players tap on the way to the playing field or simply a personal note for you individually in your locker, at

(*continued*)

(*Continued*)

your desk, or in your car. The choice of having the right mindset is a daily and sometimes hourly activity. We all need to be reminded consistently.

Try this

☞ Create a list of what you are thankful for. Use this list as the catalyst to choose to be successful within your work and in life. Life is a gift; how you use it is your choice.

Try this

☞ Create a covenant within your team, department, or organization to remain positive no matter the circumstances. Place the covenant either within the contracts, in handbooks, or on a sign for all to see—and remember.

Attitude 3.3:
Desire

The starting point of all achievement is desire.

—Napoleon Hill

There must be a relentless resolve to carry out the execution of the Experience, and sometimes you have to fight for it. There are far too many people who will both knowingly and unknowingly work against you and your team, while you attempt to create the Exceptional. You will see complacency, laziness, jealousy, or anything else that is the enemy of excellence all around you. And don't think that your customers will not take notice. *In a recent InteliSpend study, we learned that 41 percent of customers are loyal to a brand or company because they consistently notice a positive employee attitude, while 68 percent of customers defect from a brand or company because of negative employee attitude.* The relentless resolve to be the best at what you do and to create the best possible Experience in and for your organization is the only way you can achieve the Exceptional.

> *In a recent InteliSpend study, we learned that 41 percent of customers are loyal to a brand or company because they consistently notice a positive employee attitude, while 68 percent of customers defect from a brand or company because of negative employee attitude.*

Desire Is Contagious

We have all heard the old saying "You can lead a horse to water, but you can't make him drink." We've added a little addendum to the old saying: you *can* put some salt in his oats, which makes him thirsty. Our responsibility as leaders and our job as both employees and human beings is to help manifest the *thirst*, the *desire*, in others that creates the drive needed to succeed. The first step to doing this is having the level of desire in your own heart that you would want to place in the people around you. Even though you can't change people, you *can* inspire them—and that is the most anyone can reasonably do.

Desire can build momentum and become viral. When people get excited and begin to develop the muscles of execution and the resolve to continue to repeat the little things that makes an Experience Exceptional, it begins to spread to others in the organization. This is most likely the greatest ingredient for you internal Ambassadors: the art of creating contagious desire. However, remember this: *momentum* is different from *motivation*.

Two things we know about motivation are:

1. You cannot motivate other people.
2. People do things for *their* reasons, not yours.

If I put a gun to your head and demand you take some action, that isn't motivation; that is coercion. Motivation is *only* self-induced. However, you can build momentum through contagious desire and the right Attitude. Once you build enough momentum that everyone catches on and joins the movement, even the most discontented sourpusses will not want to be left out of the fun.

Passion and Purpose

We don't refer to passion as that romantic feeling here, but rather the gut-felt enthusiasm and excitement within you. It is the "who you are" and "what you stand for" that are unleashed through passion. Passion is the driving force that causes most people to excel.

Passion is that deep conviction and pride in what you do. The old principle is true today more than ever: "Look for something you love to do, and you will never work a day in your life." If you find something that fills you with passion and purpose, you will instinctively pour yourself into it. That is why Steve Jobs and Thomas Edison worked 20-hour days. To them, it was no longer work; they were simply doing what they loved to do. Their passion for their inventions and work gave them the purpose and value to do what they loved.

Bernie Marcus and Arthur Blank were executives with the Handy Dan Home Improvement stores in Southern California who were both fired. Rather than sticking their heads in the sand and giving up on their passion, they envisioned the creation of a home improvement store that would be nationwide and bigger than any other. Sticking to their values and their culture of customer service and valuing others, Blank and Marcus led Home Depot to become the first home improvement company to reach $30 billion in sales.

Walt Disney's first commercial success was Oswald the Lucky Rabbit in 1927. Although Walt had created Oswald, he failed to copyright the character and did not own the rights to Oswald. Walt traveled from Los Angeles to New York City by train, only to discover that his manager had stolen Oswald and all the artists for himself, leaving Walt high and dry. But instead of sinking into anger and despair, Walt sent a telegram to his partner and older brother, Roy, stating: "Don't worry; everything is okay. I will give the details when I arrive."

Walt's three-day journey back to Los Angeles could have been the longest of his life had he not been an eternal optimist. He pulled out his sketchpad and started creating a new character, but this time he decided not to show it to anyone until he had procured all the rights. In 1928, Walt introduced Mickey Mouse to the world via "Steamboat Willie."

Mickey Mouse would become an instant success—while Oswald has faded into oblivion.

Walt was once quoted as saying, "Everyone falls down. Getting back up is how you learn how to walk." If Walt had never lost the rights to Oswald, he might never have felt the need to create a new character and we would not have Mickey, Minnie, Pluto, or Goofy. He would probably not have had the money to build the studios and the parks. *Cinderella*, *Snow White*, and *The Lion King* would never have been created and you would never have heard of Disneyland or Disney World. Sometimes our failures are the best things that can happen to us. When the chips are down, that is when true desire shines the brightest.

Quotient Question

Is there a desire and a relentless resolve to create an Exceptional Experience for each client and customer?

Actionables

Desire is what adds purpose, drive, and direction to everything you do.

Try this

☞ Write down three specific areas personally or within the organization in which you see a lack of desire. Work with others to create an action plan on what you will do to improve them.

Try this

☞ Find the three most negative people within your organization and make it a weekly habit to encourage, inspire, and support them.

(*continued*)

(*Continued*)

Try this

☞ Have everyone make a list of the top three things they are most passionate about in life. Next ask them to correlate those passions with the execution of the organization's customer Experience.

Attitude 3.4:
Yes

The big question is whether you are going to be able to say a hearty yes to your adventure.

—Joseph Campbell

A "Yes" mentality is one of the most powerful tools you can have at your disposal. For Bruce, working for Disney World was both exciting and stressful at the same time. It's not always easy being "the happiest place on earth." The difference maker for Disney's cast members was that many of the managers worked to maintain a "Yes" mentality and a can-do Attitude that quickly became infectious. Those who exude a positive spirit are able to create positive outcomes, which makes work and service more enjoyable for everyone.

When those around you, your coworkers in the trenches, are choosing to look at the bright side of their work, happiness can supersede the negatives we experience every day. The same goes for our reaction to our customers. Is "No" a plausible answer to anything in your organization? *A recent KISSmetrics blog for analytics and marketing stated that in a single year, the financial sector alone lost $44 billion due to poor customer service.* What are the "No's" in your organization costing you? As long as no one could be hurt or fired and as long as you are staying

A recent KISSmetrics blog for analytics and marketing stated that in a single year, the financial sector alone lost $44 billion due to poor customer service.

within the realm of physics and the known laws of time and space, everything should be a "Yes."

Bruce used to work with a performer named Fred at Walt Disney World, who was one of the most cynical and negative people he ever encountered. Fred had a complaint and reason to whine about anything and everyone. People always commented, "Well, that's Fred!" What was interesting was how everyone accepted Fred as part of the group, yet didn't buy in to his negative and critical comments about everything. Everyone else got along great and weathered many a storm because the majority of the cast members took on a "Yes" and a can-do mindset, even in the midst of Fred's negativity.

Disney cast members often get accused of having a Pollyanna outlook and disposition about life. It's not as if these people do not go back to the real world every day and have life waiting for them, nor are they interminably positive, either. Most cast members at Disney merely recognize that they have a choice: to view life positively and choose the upside or to be the victim and always have a reason to complain and be negative. Disney has been very effective at finding, hiring, and training the right people the right way.

In his book *One Minute Service* (DC Press, 2009), Bruce discusses the difference between having a positive Attitude and a negative Attitude.

Defining Attitudes

- **Negative Attitude:** Those individuals who focus on all the negatives of work, who tend to be down about everything, who continually whine and complain, who criticize customers and coworkers, who take their frustration out on others

(continued)

(*Continued*)

verbally, and who feel like victims, dwelling on problems rather than focusing on solutions.

- **Positive Attitude:** Those who take pride in their work, strive for excellence, continually give their best, encourage others, find positive things to say about their work and their coworkers, and continually strive to improve and give their best to the company and those they work with.

Eliminate the Negatives

The problem with negativity is that it is literally all in the mind. When negative thoughts begin to creep into your subconscious, they often morph and manifest themselves into your Attitudes, which become your behaviors. Thoughts are powerful because they have the ability to influence every other aspect of your Attitude. It is impossible to have two thoughts simultaneously. So, as long as you give the negative ones credence, this is what you will dwell on—and what will become manifest in your thoughts and actions. The key is to replace the negative thoughts with positive, productive thoughts.

It really doesn't matter what others think of you. You can't control what others think, so you might as well take the approach that what they think is really none of your business. Concentrate instead on controlling the things over which you have direct influence. First and foremost are your thoughts. For years, we've heard that most things we worry about never happen. Researchers at the University of Cincinnati have found that a full *85 percent* of the things we worry about never come true. Why spend so much of our energy there?

It's so easy to say "No." Anyone can be negative and critical or cynical. The challenge is to create a culture where "Yes" is the rule instead of the exception. Constructive thinking is the enemy of "No" and the ally of "Yes."

Quotient Question

Does every employee make a conscientious effort to avoid the word "No" and to seek ways to say "Yes" and ways to positively resolve every situation?

Actionables

The ability to say "Yes" is a door opener to happiness. "Yes" offers the freedom to positively impact others and enable them to experience the Exceptional.

Try this

☞ Once a month, have a "Yes" day. Attempt to say "Yes" to every question, every response, and each opportunity that comes your way.

Try this

☞ Count your "No's." Display them if necessary. There are times when they bring about a necessary warning to customers or clients, but by counting the "No," "can't," and "won't" responses, you become aware of negative interactions.

Try this

☞ Once a week, have a "Highlights Exercise." This is the opportunity for coworkers to tell their tales of Exceptional Experiences—the times when they made someone's day or were the hero of a moment when the Experience was threatened.

Attitude 3.5:
Happiness

The secret ingredients to true happiness? Decisive optimism and personal responsibility.

—Amy Leigh Mercree

Being an optimist and therefore possessing true happiness often boils down to the way you talk to yourself. Optimists believe that their own actions result in positive things happening, that they are responsible for their own happiness, and that they can expect more good things to happen in the future. Optimists don't blame themselves when bad things happen. They view bad events as results of something outside of themselves.

Unfortunately, negativity comes naturally to most of us. In our experience, we've found that it is much easier to be negative than it is to be positive. There is some evidence to the expression "Misery loves company." Have you ever met a person who just seems to have a heavy, black cloud that follows him or her everywhere—someone to whom one bad thing after another happens? Usually, there is a reason for it: these individuals are looking for and expect disaster, and often have a "woe is me" mindset. It is entirely true that the things you look for and expect in life tend to come true. So, if you are always expecting to fail, to receive a low score on a test, or to lose most of the time, you will usually fulfill your predictions.

Northwestern University did a study on happiness in the 1970s. The bad news the researchers discovered is that 50 percent of your happiness is genetic, so there is nothing you can do about that part. However, the good news is 50 percent of your happiness is derived from your daily behavior and how you think about and go about helping others. The bottom line is that being happy is ultimately *your choice*.

Yet, the opposite is also true. Those people who seem to win in life usually have a very positive outlook. They expect to do well on a test, they expect to succeed, they expect get the promotion or a part in the play, and they generally expect to win at whatever they do. We have asked hundreds of people who attend our seminars: "How many of you would consider yourself to be a positive, optimistic person most of the time today?" Only about 30 percent of hands go up. Then we ask those who raised their hands, "Have you always been a positive person your entire life or have you had to work at it?" Most will say they have had to fight and work diligently in order to stay positive. Hara Estroff Marano, editor in chief of *Psychology Today* magazine, reported that the average person generates 25,000 to 50,000 thoughts per day. You might as well make them happy ones. Being a positive, happy person is a deliberate decision on your part.

You Can't Hide Happiness

My mother loves to tell the following story about a young Disney cast member she met at the Magic Kingdom one evening. It was 1981, and Lyndal and Gary Church were exiting the park with their then-six-year-old son Brian (me), when they saw a young man who was whistling as he made his way to one of the stage doors. My mother asked him why he was so happy. His response was simply: "I love working here. If I could stay here all night I would. I honestly never want to leave. It's magical, isn't it?" The young man's Attitude was authentic; it was true happiness and it was as magical as Disney World itself.

You really can't hide happiness. You also cannot fabricate it. Happiness is a state of being that is brought on by a certain optimism and appreciation of your ecosystem. This component of the Disney Experience is one that is seldom replicated but something we should all strive to acquire.

Creating the Happiness Experience

As we have said before, it's not easy for the people at Disney to create a "happiness destination" or "the happiest place on earth." In fact, it's impossible without that single foundational ingredient. Happiness is a state of mind that we must all work at. It does not come naturally to most people. Happiness is an atmosphere that Ambassadors create. The moment you step onto a Disney property or into a venue or facility, you can observe and feel the vibe being emitted. The commitment to the happiness atmosphere is the secret to creating the happiness experience. This difficult task begins with the right Attitude, is supported by training and encouragement, and is then pulled together with an awareness of and special attention to the atmosphere. You can—you must—make the choice to be happy!

Quotient Question

Do employees and their coworkers focus on being positive and grateful, and are they creating an environment of happiness?

Actionables

What is terrific about happiness is that it truly is a choice that lies within you, regardless of circumstances.

Try this

☞ Put a physical and emotional smile on your face *the first 30 minutes* of every day. Your mind is a neutral instrument;

(continued)

(*Continued*)

it cannot differentiate between real and imagined. To physically smile and dwell on the positives of work and customers for 30 minutes will change your frame of mind, your outlook, and your mood.

Try this

☞ When something negative has happened or is about to happen, isolate the issue; make a mental mark of the item and then prepare yourself and others around you to expect the outcome to be in your favor. Watch what happens!

Try this

☞ Reflect on the wins! Note the made sales goals, the closed account, the new relationship. Do not dwell on them for too long, but just as we need to be cognizant of the losses, we have to take the time to celebrate the triumphs.

Attitude 3.6:
Optimism

Optimism is the faith that leads to achievement. Nothing can be done without hope and confidence.

—Helen Keller

It's almost impossible to understate the power of positive thinking. Optimism—derived from the Latin word *optimus*, which means "best"—is hopefulness and confidence about the future or the successful outcome of something. As we identified in the previous sub-Principle on happiness, truly optimistic people always tend to see the good in their future and in turn to anticipate good things. They have a knack for thinking that everything will turn out in their favor—and even if something doesn't, they still continue to believe that all things will work together for an ultimately beneficial ending.

While happiness and optimism are certainly related, there is an interesting difference between them. Happiness is a state of being that can exist only on the other side of optimism. You cannot have one without the other. If you truly want to create an Experience filled with happiness, you must first infuse optimism and its thought agents, the eternal optimists.

The Eternal Optimist

Walt Disney was known as an eternal optimist. Without his Attitude, there would have been no way for him and his partners to build a place

152

that was and is synonymous with Exceptional Experiences. He was famous for sayings like "All of our dreams can come true if we have the courage to pursue them," "It's kind of fun to do the impossible," and "If you can dream it, you can do it!"

Though he was also a perfectionist, Walt Disney's infectious optimism attracted people in droves to follow his vision and dreams. How many of us can look at what feels like a daunting task and see it as a fun challenge?

Optimism Is an Inside Job

Another beneficial aspect of being an optimistic person is that research shows that people who are generally optimistic thinkers most of the time are sick less often and also tend to live longer. The ability to build up the immune system and to handle stress leads to fewer heart attacks. In contrast, those who are generally pessimistic often tend to think that "the world is out to get me" and to shoulder the blame for everything bad that happens to them. Even when positive things happen to them, they tend to brush them off as anomalies and give no credence to those events.

Optimists often look for the positive in any situation. Even when a disaster occurs, they tend to view it as a one-time event and move on with a hearty "Next!" *According to a study administered by the Metropolitan Life Insurance Company, its salespeople who had higher optimism scores on a behavioral science test sold 37 percent more life insurance in their first year in the business.* There is no doubting that there is a direct correlation between optimism and success.

> *According to a study administered by the Metropolitan Life Insurance Company, its salespeople who had higher optimism scores on a behavioral science test sold 37 percent more life insurance in their first year in the business.*

Your Thinking Is the Culprit—or the Cure

It really is how you think and what you tend to dwell on that determine whether you are a pessimist or an optimist. If you are one to constantly kick yourself over mistakes or failures due to things you've said or done, then you are most likely a pessimist. Optimism helps you think, feel, and see the world and life differently. Most of us are not born optimists; we have to work at it—very hard. The key is to stop being satisfied with negativity and pessimism.

In order to think positively, you must eliminate negative thinking patterns. According to the Mayo Clinic, these negative tendencies include four cognitive thought patterns:

1. **Filtering** refers to psychologically screening out the encouraging aspects of real-life situations.
2. **Personalizing** means blaming yourself when something bad happens.
3. **Catastrophizing** is expecting the worst possible outcome in any situation.
4. **Polarizing** is defining failure as any result short of perfection.

Fight to eliminate these within yourself and within your organization, and you will not only see the level of the Experience increase, but you and your coworkers will also begin to see a higher quality of work life.

Perception Is the Key

A story is told of twin boys who had completely different personalities. One was the consummate pessimist; the other, the eternal optimist. A psychologist asked permission to try an experiment with the two boys to see how each would react to a very negative situation.

On their birthday, a pile of horse manure was placed in a room. The boys entered after being told there was a present in the room for each of them. The pessimistic twin immediately ran out, yelling at his mom and everyone else about the awful trick they had played on him.

No one heard anything from the second twin, the optimistic one. After a while, the psychologist became concerned and entered the room. Hearing the boy inside the manure pile, the psychologist asked, "What are you doing?" The young optimist called out, "With all this manure, there must be a pony in here somewhere!" Now, that's optimism!

Quotient Question

Is there a spirit of optimism within the organization and with regard to the ability to execute an Exceptional Experience?

Actionables

Optimism is what provides the hope to go on and to visualize a better today and tomorrow.

Try this

☞ Create one positive, powerful affirmation that defines who you are, what you are going to achieve, how you will approach the future, and what you will give in order to be successful. Repeat this affirmation daily, and it will change your today and your tomorrow. This works for individuals and organizations alike.

Try this

☞ Just as you derive a self-talk, it is equally important to incorporate a team talk. Create one as a group, organization, or department that defines you when times get tough. The way you talk about the team corporately has a direct impact on how you will all feel and perform.

(continued)

(Continued)

Try this

☞ You cannot make people be happy or positive. However, you can influence them through a positive environment. Anytime you hear someone make a negative comment, criticize someone, or be derogatory about anyone, encourage the person to be positive. Also, give others the authority to stop you on the spot and question your negative thinking as well.

Attitude 3.7:
Expectations

High expectations are the key to everything.

—Sam Walton

We have discovered after working with thousands of employees over the past 20 years that there are three basic keys to providing ongoing relational service. Customers want us to:

1. **Seek**—understand their wants and needs
2. **Set**—form consistent and executable expectations
3. **Solidify**—personalize their service

Seek

Setting expectations requires creating two-way communication with others. First, it is essential that you have a clear picture of what they want, need, and expect before you can effectively help them. If we were a care provider in a hospital and someone had come in to have his or her gallbladder removed, the first thing we would do is ascertain what type of care and support the person expected from us. We would ask questions about the comfort, visitors, quietness, food, and any concerns that the patient might have. And we would be taking meticulous notes the entire time, so we would have a record of the patient's expectations.

Set

Next, we would tell the patient what he or she could expect during the hospital stay, including how the procedure and recovery would go. If virtually everything happens just as it was presented, wouldn't we have a very satisfied patient leaving the hospital? It works the same way in your business. People don't want surprises; they want to know what is going to happen, and then they want consistency in the delivery.

Solidify

Finally, people want to receive personalized service. The first order of business is to create a set of expectations from and for customers that lets them know they are welcome and important to your business. Without them, your company would cease to exist.

Our primary focus in creating *The Experience* advantage is to deliver Exceptional customer service to each and every customer. You do that by understanding what their expectations are and then proceeding to exceed those expectations.

Recently, Bruce was in a nice supermarket near his home in Tennessee when he noticed a pattern. Apparently, the management of the store had conditioned the employees to greet each customer who passed by in the aisle. The first employee greeted Bruce with "How ya doin'?"; the second, "How are you doing?"; the third, "How are you doing?"; and the fourth, "Hi, how are you doing?" Bruce applauded the managers for encouraging every single employee to greet and to acknowledge each customer passing by. However, they failed to encourage any originality or personalization in their greeting. After a short while, the phrase "How are you doing?" became a plastic mantra that meant very little.

What management should have done is go one step further and have every employee look each customer in the eye as they passed and greet them with their own personal greeting, such as "Good morning," "May I help you?," "Are you finding everything?," "How is your day going?," and a myriad of other greetings. The key is to set our expectations that "We provide personalized attention to everyone." That is what every customer wants and ultimately what they expect from you.

The Ripple Effect

As a thought experiment, let's say one of us is a new customer visiting your business for the first time and several of your employees are having a bad day. It just happens that the first three employees that we meet in your store are rude, cold, and abrasive. What do you think we will expect from that point on? We would be looking for the same from each of the other employees in the business: rude, cold, and abrasive. Even if we were to discover that the next five are excellent, we would anticipate that others would be rude, cold, and abrasive at some point.

According to the American Express Global Customer Service Barometer, consumers in the United Kingdom feel that companies are meeting their customer service expectations only 62 percent of the time. In the United States, the number comes in significantly lower at only 8 percent. When our first Experiences are negative and those poor Experiences are reinforced, then they create a template for what to expect from that point on. It appears there are a lot of mismanaged expectations and quite a bit of experiential underachievement in the global marketplace. That is why Impressions, Connections, and Attitudes are so critical to the exposure the customer has to our business. The ripple effect looms large, and the opportunity is there to differentiate yourself and your organization. Expect success, and then train employees and prepare your customers to expect an Exceptional Experience.

Quotient Question

Do the employees of the organization create and then meet expectations of a positive Experience for the clients and customers?

Actionables

People will always stretch or diminish what they accomplish based on their expectations that others set for them.

Try this

☞ Set a goal to ask five customers each day what they expect from the services or products you deliver, and also give them specific examples of what they can expect from you and the company.

Try this

☞ Actively listen with comments such as: "Let me make certain I understand you," "Please allow me to repeat what you said," and "Is this what you meant?" Active listening is essential to understanding, setting, and also delivering on the expectations of others.

Try this

☞ Once each week, take a mental inventory of what your expectations are as to the level of the Experience that should be provided. Then map your expectations with those of your customers and client base. Are they the same? How will you make them correlate more? The more you and your team become students of the Experience, the more enhanced the Experience becomes.

Attitude 3.8:
Persistence

Ambition is the path to success. Persistence is the vehicle you arrive in.
—Bill Bradley

The people who drive the Experience must continue to improve in all facets of work. The key is not to fold when there is a crack, but to fix, to reengineer, and to improve. It is critical to realize that the Experience is never finished. If an Exceptional Experience were easy to create and replicate, everyone would do it—and the Toxic level for American companies would be much lower than it currently is. It *should* be hard; that is what makes it so rare and valuable. And you *should* strive to bask in the sun of one of the few organizations that can grasp the Exceptional.

F.E.A.R

Fear is the greatest enemy of innovation and excellence. It is what causes many people to give up on their way to being Exceptional. Persistence is partly about making the good great and the great even greater; but most of what makes up persistence is the ability and focus to fight through the pain of change and failure to progress up the ladder of success.

We think of fear as an acronym—(F)alse (E)vidence (A)ppearing (R)eal. Most of us see challenges as a giant mountain when we should focus on only that day's climb. Driving an incredible client deliverable and service offering is a very difficult, long-term challenge. Depending on what level of the five levels of the Experience you begin your journey, the mountain can seem impossible to summit. Whether you are an owner or an employee, do not let your own fear of hard work, failure, and opposition keep you from taking small bites out of the mountain climb and ultimately driving your organization toward the Exceptional.

The Greatest Failure

Here is an interesting question: *who was the greatest failure in history?* We'll give you a few hints: he failed 14,000 times to invent Latex. He failed 10,000 times to invent the incandescent lightbulb. Now, I don't know about you, but I'm not aware of anyone else who has failed at anything 24,000 times—and those were just two of his experiments. *Over the course of his life, he failed at more than 250,000 attempts at various inventions. Yet he is the most prolific inventor ever known. He patented 1,093 different inventions, including the lightbulb, the stock ticker tape, the phonograph, and the microphone. His name was Thomas Edison.*

A reporter asked him one time, "Mr. Edison, how does it feel to have failed 10,000 times in your present venture?" Edison replied, "Young man, since you are just getting started in life, let me give you something that will benefit you the rest of your life. I have never failed at *anything* 10,000 times. I have, however, found 10,000 ways that it will successfully . . . *not work!*" His secret was Attitude, and his key was perseverance—which happen to be your keys to success as well.

Six Keys to Persistence

Persistence is a muscle that must be trained and developed over time. The mere definition of persistence is the continuance of a certain effort even after its cause has been removed. When we are working toward a specific goal, in this case the Exceptional Experience, the cause should never be removed; however, the energy, the emotion, and the "why" often fade from our minds while in pursuit of the goal. This defining moment is when persistence shines and we find our cerebral persistence muscles that bring us through the lulls of the journey.

Persistence is imperative to anyone chasing excellence in any endeavor. We have discovered six keys to building persistence muscles:

1. **Reason—know the why.** When our mission, purpose, and goal are fixed in our minds and held there, they saturate our entire subconscious until they influence us to take physical actions to achieve of our goal.

2. **Passion—know the desire.** The strength of our desire—how badly we want to achieve this goal—is often answered by the question "Why?" And our answer to this question will be our reminder when we have a failure or are frustrated by disappointment.

3. **Knowledge—know your skills.** We may have a goal, but not the skill or knowledge needed to achieve our goal. As we gain the knowledge, skills, and experience, we are able to see the possibilities of achievement.

4. **Action—take the initiative.** Taking the first step moves us toward results. Once we stop procrastinating and start acting, it is easier to stay committed and keep the ball rolling.

5. **Support—cooperate with others.** Having people in our circle of influence who know what our goal is and who have similar goals can be a big support to us achieving our goal. They can spark our imagination and encourage us in times when we are lacking motivation.

6. **Commitment—never give up.** Building persistence muscles is not a comfortable process. The process comes down to the extra rep where you build that next level of capacity for the journey. The keys to building persistence are circular, and the commitment to finish the pursuit of the goal is reflected in the reason why you started in the beginning.

Pursuit of the Mundane Edge

In the early 2000s I worked for a world-class money manager in Boston called Putnam Investments. The president of distribution at the time was a man named Billy Connolly, and he had a saying. He would challenge the sales force and proclaim that they were in the "pursuit of the mundane edge." Now, some may confuse the word *mundane* with monotonous or boring; however, this is not the definition of mundane. Mundane means "of this world or common." The challenge was to make excellence a habit so that the sales force's impeccable execution would be so repetitious that it would become the norm and not extraordinary at all. That excellence would become the rule and not the exception. Putnam was able to build one of the finest sales forces in the world, and in the year 2000 outsold almost every other retail mutual fund company on the planet.

Ask yourself this question: Are you in the "pursuit of the mundane edge"—or are you allowing F.E.A.R., complacency, opposition, or failure get in the way of creating a culture or organization that consistently pushes for the Exceptional? This is what separates Disney from the rest of the world. Not only does Disney hire, prepare, train, and execute for the Exceptional; it is able to sustain it. As we have been able to talk with Dick Nunis, one of the cerebral architects of Disney, he has told us that it was no small matter fighting to build the "happiest place on earth." Persistence was the key, and this is why the Disney Experience is like no other.

Quotient Question

Is there a "never give up" mindset around excellence, and is there a consistent effort to improve and to reengineer the Experience?

Actionables

The ability to never give up, to press on toward the mark, is what typically separates successes from failures.

Try this

☞ The next time you are fearful, meet the fear head-on; write it down so you can isolate what you think you are afraid of, and then attack it with a vengeance. Be relentless in breaking it down and conquering it, once and for all. Do not attempt this alone; share this with others, as they may have the same anxieties as you.

Try this

☞ Each Friday, look back over the past week at something you did that was unsuccessful or misunderstood. Analyze what went wrong, and create an action plan to "never make the same mistake twice." These little acknowledgments are pure gold in your personal or corporate growth track.

Try this

☞ Whether as a team or individually, establish three specific goals that are meaningful to you. Write down why each is important, how you intend to achieve it, and why you will never allow anything or anyone to deter you from your mission. These goals do you no good in a drawer. Post them where you and others can see them.

Attitude 3.9:
Ownership

There is no delight in owning anything unshared.

—Lucius Annaeus Seneca

Does everyone in your organization *own* the Experience? Is it an option for them to not take ownership of the deliverable or service offering? Do you ever hear the words "That's not my job" or "I didn't do it"? We all know that creating an extraordinary Experience for others is a team effort. The question—and the quest—involves figuring out how to get everyone attitudinally united and involved in making it a reality.

My previous book, *Relationship Momentum*, relates an interesting story about famed explorer Hernán Cortés and the lost City of Gold. Many will recall from history class that Cortés was on a quest for a treasure beyond anyone's wildest dreams. For 600 years, numerous would-be conquerors had tried to capture the City of Gold, but every one of them failed. Cortés was a wealthy Spanish landowner. He studied why each of the conquerors had failed and realized that the City of Gold was always a side trip for them and never their main purpose. So, he sold his land and his farms and purchased 11 boats with his own money. He then selected crews for his boats with the express purpose of conquering the new land.

When Cortés arrived on foreign soil, his men practiced drills for several weeks to prepare their attack. Finally, the day came when Cortés felt his army was ready. Just before they attacked the city, Cortés called his army together for final instructions and three simple words that made all the difference: *Burn the ships!* Cortés knew that each of the other armies that had lost always had an escape route planned in the event they failed, but to Cortés, failure was not an option. He said, "Either we take the gold or we die here, and when we take the gold, we are going home in *their* ships." They fought well and won their prize.

What "ships" in your organization do you need to burn? These are the things keeping you or your teammates from total commitment to be all in. Success favors the all-or-nothing mentality. When we become totally committed and each of us takes on the Attitude of ownership and personal responsibility, a funny thing happens—we usually win.

One issue with many organizations today is that the employees have a hard time feeling as if they own a piece of the mission. *In fact, according to InteliSpend research, only 40 percent of employees are well informed about their company's goals, strategy, and tactics to begin with.* In a world where we can only figuratively burn the ships, how can anyone expect appropriate Attitudes if the employees are not well enough informed to feel like owners of the mission?

> *In fact, according to InteliSpend research, only 40 percent of employees are well informed about their company's goals, strategy, and tactics to begin with.*

Creating Opportunity

The Japanese grow a tree called the bonsai tree. It is perfectly formed and beautiful, but it will grow to only 10 to 12 inches at most. Yet it may live for 50 years. In California are giant trees called sequoias, the tallest in the world. In fact, the General Sherman reaches to 272 feet high and measures 79 feet in circumference. This tree is so large that if it were cut down, it could supply enough wood to build 35 five-room houses.

At one time, these two trees were the exact same size. So what happened? When the bonsai was just a seedling, it was pulled from the ground and its taproot and several other feeder roots were cut, thus stunting its growth. The sequoias grew in fertile soil and were surrounded by other sequoias. The root system of the sequoia is only about five feet deep; so where does it derive its strength? Instead of sending its taproots down deep, it sends them out hundreds of feet to intertwine with root systems of other sequoias, and together they serve to stabilize each other.

From the story of the bonsai and the sequoia, we find two principles that can change our lives. Unlike the bonsai, in order to reach your full potential, you need to go deep and tap into all the talent, wisdom, and experience you can along the way. This is the essence of ownership. It is a common goal, a common culture, and a common commitment to excellence in the path to the goal.

Like the sequoias, you need to intertwine your talents and skills with like-minded people who can strengthen you and pull you through the tough times of life. We all need others around us in order to succeed. We always chuckle when we hear the phrase "a self-made millionaire." Unless you are printing counterfeit money, there is no such thing. All successful people were surrounded by others who helped to inspire fresh ideas in them, who challenged and coached them, and who may have funded projects along the way; bankers and manufacturers who help them build their dream; and customers who purchased the product or service, and salespeople who sold that product or service.

Bruce recalls the original story of Walt Disney. When Walt first started drawing, he borrowed his uncle's garage for a studio. His uncle lent Walt $500 with the clear understanding that as soon as Walt made enough money, he was to pay him back.

It has been documented that had Walt's uncle decided to invest that $500 into Walt's new company instead of requiring Walt to pay it back, that amount would be worth over $1 billion today. There are two morals to that story: (1) ownership, albeit with more risk, often returns a higher yield than a loan, and (2) no one has ever done anything completely on their own. It took an investment or a sense of ownership from others to make the magic happen. Opportunities are all around us if we will take ownership and pour ourselves fully into what we do, and if we will utilize the talent, wisdom, and coaching of others to help us succeed.

Quotient Question

How well do employees take ownership of the Experience and personal responsibility for the success of their team, their department, and the organization?

Actionables

The ability to act as though you own the Experience and any opportunities or problems is the pride that separates averageness from excellence.

Try this

☞ Make sure that everyone in the organization understands the mission at hand. An Attitude of ownership begins with familiarity and solidarity in the goals and initiatives of the team, never before. If you want an Exceptional Experience, make sure everyone understands why and is incentivized accordingly.

Try this

☞ Be willing to apologize when there is a problem, but do not blame others or make excuses. Your customer doesn't care about your excuses or even whose fault it was, only about the results and the eventual outcome. The next time there is

(continued)

(Continued)

a service recovery issue, you take personal ownership to resolve the problem immediately. This only helps the team, and it is a fantastic example to those around you.

Try this

☞ Once a week, have a team meeting to discuss successes and glitches that have occurred during the past week. Repeat the Great and eliminate the Toxic. Use these as guidelines on how to build an Exceptional customer Experience.

Attitude 3.10:
Illumination

Whatever you vividly imagine, ardently desire, sincerely believe and enthusiastically act upon . . . must inevitably come true.

—Paul J. Meyer

What illuminates your potential? What drives and inspires you to be better, to improve, to give your best, to separate yourself from the rest of the pack—in short, to be great? Where does *your* inspiration come from? To some it is the passion to learn; to others it is the opportunity to grow and make a difference in others. To some it is the random acts of kindness they do *without* anyone being aware of their efforts, and to some it is making people happy and fulfilling their dreams.

The key to inspiration and illumination can be found in this simple quote: *"Love what you do, or do what you love."* Those who are truly fulfilled do one of two things: they pour themselves fully into the work they do regardless of whether they enjoy the work *or* they find work that suits them where they do what they were designed to do.

As we stated earlier, you cannot change other people, so any improvement, any growth, must germinate within a person. You can, however, inspire others to change. Transforming yourself can give others the motivation and desire to want to improve their own situations. Your responsibility is to be the example, coach, and catalyst that incites a change that others desire to follow.

The underlying goal of this book is to help you create and execute a higher level of Experience for your customers and clients. As we have discussed, the glue and the mortar to the Exceptional Experience is the Attitude behind it. *According to a recent Customers 2020 Report, by the year 2020, customer Experience will overtake price and product as the key brand differentiator.* The need for creating and replicating a positive Experience is greater than ever before. But don't do it for profits and promotions alone. Do it because your customers deserve better.

> *According to a recent Customers 2020 Report, by the year 2020, customer Experience will overtake price and product as the key brand differentiator.*

A Battle for the Mind

First and foremost, you need to recognize that Attitude is all your choice. You alone control how and what you feel. Opinions matter, of course; that is a central lesson of this book. However, it is your opinion of yourself that matters first and matters the most. How you perceive today and what you achieve tomorrow are totally yours; in other words, it's your choice.

As an example, take the writing of this book. There have been numerous moving parts. The researching and testing of over 500 companies alone was a daunting task. Combine that with the time and effort to build the algorithms and the Experience Quotient, compounded with the cerebral feat of having to collaborate as two very strong-willed authors, made the mountain almost impossible to climb. There were many times when we wanted to give up. However, we believed in the cause and the message, and we believed in ourselves and also in each other and that we could pull it off.

This is not the first book for either of us. However, we both have been writing for years but with very limited success. I actually have written or started writing six books over the past decade with only two of them being published. Life is a battle; you have to fight for your dreams and your goals. We believe in ourselves and in the reasons why we create ideas and challenges for others. The choice is ours with regard to ultimate success or failure, and the choice is yours as to whether you can achieve the Exceptional.

Worry, Fear, and Negativity

Few things kill success faster than worry, fear, and negativity. Worry will do absolutely nothing to improve your situation, so worrying about something that will most likely not come to pass is a waste of your time and talent.

The best approach for handling fear is not to avoid it, but rather to attack it. Bruce recently witnessed a psychological test about ophidiophobia, fear of snakes. He said how, at the beginning, four women were terrified of the snakes and froze when they saw them. But, by the end of the program, each of the four picked up the snakes and was able to hold them. The key to fear is to face whatever it is head-on; as you do, you gradually begin to conquer whatever the fear is. The number one fear in the United States is not bankruptcy, death, or divorce, but public speaking. How do you ever conquer public speaking? By speaking at any and every opportunity you can. Doing so helps you see that the thing you're so afraid of really isn't that bad—and you gradually conquer what was holding you back.

Negativity is very much the same issue. As we have noted, it is several times easier to be negative than it is to be positive, which means being negative just comes naturally to most of us. Famed author and motivational speaker Zig Ziglar has discovered that negativity is a bad habit, and the only way to change a habit is to replace it with a new one and consistently insert the new habit each and every time you are about to revert back to the old one. The only way to change the habit of negativity is to alter what and how you think by replacing the negative thoughts with positive ideas, outcomes, and solutions.

Fight the Average Undertow

One of the great aspects of the Disney Experience is that visitors get to release their imaginations to become whatever they want to be while they are in a Disney park. Many executives have left with a new vision that has revitalized their businesses, their people, and even their products. Whether it's the Illumination fireworks show or the way that the different sections of the park are run, many leaders come to Disney World to find inspiration, as well as enjoyment. It's hard to visit the Magic Kingdom and *not* leave inspired with a new perspective.

Customers want exciting, fresh, new, innovative, and fun Experiences—and only imagination can help you deliver that. Whether you hold the title of owner, president, manager, salesperson, shipping clerk, delivery driver, or custodian, you are the head of "You Incorporated." If you are always willing to settle for being Average or mediocre, you will *never* achieve the levels and the rewards you have the potential to achieve. Executing an Exceptional Experience will take courage and illumination; you must embrace the right Attitude and fight the undertow of the mediocre. There is a treasure that lies on the other side of Average. Unfortunately, only 40 percent of American companies know what that treasure is. Perhaps you have encountered the spoils before. The treasure is wind in your sails, incredible growth rates, profitable quarters, excited board members, and, most important, happy employees and customers!

Quotient Question

Do the leaders of the organization practice what they preach, and do the employees exude confidence in their ability and will to create a great Experience?

Actionables

Never allow yourself to settle for less than excellence. It is what differentiates you from others.

Try this

☞ Place sticky notes in obvious places—computer screen, back of a door, your bathroom at home, calendar—with a three- to five-word phrase or power quote to reinforce excellence.

Try this

☞ Work diligently to eliminate bad habits (primarily negativity). You must begin to identify when you are heading toward negativity. Develop the cerebral muscles to notice, isolate, and then correct your negative behavior.

Try this

☞ On a sheet of paper, utilize a T chart to define what an average Experience looks like, and then compare it to what your idea of Exceptional looks like. Next, decipher the major differences between the two and design a specific action plan of how you are going to incorporate the most antithetical attributes of the two.

Chapter Seven
Principle 4: Response

Between stimulus and response there is space. In that space is our power to choose our response. In our response lies our growth and our freedom.

—Viktor E. Frankl

The Response is the point at which we find the hallmark of customer service and the Exceptional Experience. If your employees' reaction time, tone, and talent do not match up with every other aspect of an excellent Experience, everything is rendered useless. It can take vast amounts of effort to build up a relationship with a consumer, but only one negative Response to destroy it.

The previous chapters have laid the groundwork for excellence in the Experience. Responding to your clients' or customers' needs is all about delivering excellence in everything you do. You know all too well that your customers have choices about where to shop and with whom to do business. Until the past 15 years, customers would often only choose which big box store they would patronize. Nowadays, the power of the Internet and an increase in online purchasing opportunities (often at a reduced price) have made it necessary for our in-person service to be much more effective than any service over the Internet.

Lands' End and Zappos are fantastic examples of brands that have captured hearts around the world. When customers can purchase great clothes and shoes at the same (or lower) prices as they can in the big box stores *and* receive good service, only the Exceptional can protect your relationships with your consumers and clients.

Let's revisit the first two levels of "The Five Levels of the Experience" we introduced at the beginning of this book (Chapter 3). You might recall that the worst level of service is Toxic. The individuals of those companies are content delivering indifferent or even offensive service. They fail to recognize that they are on the path to lose their jobs when the company goes out of business. Customers grow tired of complaining about apathetic, disengaged, rude, and callous employees who are only interested in a paycheck.

The next level encompasses those companies that settle for Average—better than the Toxic companies, but not by much, and neither form is acceptable. Both our own internal study and a mountain of available evidence show us that you simply cannot generate new customers from those who have not received a strong or Exceptional Experience. At the very least, the level of Good should be the goal of every employee, every manager, and every executive who reads this book.

The real issue with Average is that since most people do not rise above what is expected of them and many are content to live beneath those expectations, the people and the companies that are comfortable with Average are very likely to deliver *Toxic* without realizing it. According to our model, both Toxic and Average Experiences fail to create potential Ambassadors. In fact, they often result in the opposite—the tendency for people to share negative perspectives from an unsatisfactory encounter.

Response service is dedicated to helping each employee and company to deliver excellence in every point of contact. Service is ultimately about helping, serving, and caring for others. The question is: how well do you respond to the needs of your customers and clients?

Response versus Reaction

As you might imagine, being responsive involves determining how to best respond to customers' needs. By contrast, a reaction is characterized by just "doing something." It's nice to be engaged and to throw yourself into the fray, but being responsive doesn't involve taking just *any* action; it requires taking the *right* action.

Reactions come from impulse. Even the most trained and disciplined employees often cannot control reactions. Think of the words themselves in the parlance of the medical field. When patients are doing better or improving, they are "responding" to the treatment. When they are having trouble or taking a turn for the worse, they are having a reaction.

We find a Response in between the event and the reaction. We can also think of this in terms of athletics. How many times have we heard the observation that "the game is slowing down for him"? What does this mean? It refers to the athlete seeing what is happening around him in such a way as to be able to respond more quickly than his competitors. When this happens, the game seems to come more easily to him than to anyone else, and the competition seems to be struggling to make things happen. While others are exerting more energy, the athlete is gliding along efficiently.

In order to execute the Exceptional, we must slow down the game. A Response involves thought and not simply instincts. The Response is professional, world-class—and it's at the crux of the Experience.

Hero of the Moment

The purpose of this book is to bring about a *metanoia*—a Greek term for a change in the way that you think. It all starts with a change in your thought process and then in your nomenclature and daily practices. When you do this, you automatically begin to train yourself into a new way of thinking. You must change the mind and change the vocabulary before you can change a Response. The cast members at Disney have such a specific and proprietary vocabulary because it's intentional. They are training and encouraging a way of thinking.

Response should be a frame of mind. We like to call it being the hero of the moment. Of course, it's easy to be a hero when you feel like it or if you're interacting with a friendly customer who is fun to be around. It's not so easy when the customer is in crisis mode and not acting rationally or pleasantly. *Our internal research tells us that most crises with a customer afford about 60 seconds of opportunity to defuse the situation and to pivot toward a positive interaction with your organization.* This does not mean that the issue or crisis is solved within 60 seconds, but there is definitely a brief opportunity to begin the interaction appropriately and to win back the favor of the customer or client. Your Response sets the tone and is the greatest asset you have in the Experience—because it's one of the few things that you can absolutely and unequivocally control.

> *Our internal research tells us that most crises with a customer afford about 60 seconds of opportunity to defuse the situation and to pivot toward a positive interaction with your organization.*

Willing Leaders + Engaged Employees = An Exceptional Experience

The challenge here goes back to the foundations of this book. Commit to the Exceptional Experience by changing the way that you think, and follow it with your vocabulary and your actions. Become a hero of the moment and watch the magic that happens to your relationships with your customers.

Response: Ten Disney-Inspired Non-Negotiables

Response 4.1: **Detail**
The power of being meticulous and going the extra mile.

Response 4.2: **Engagement**
The initial response sets the tone of the outcome. Problems and complaints are opportunities to bond with your client.

Response 4.3: **Urgency**
The request becomes top of mind and top of list until the consumer or client is not only satisfied but cerebrally affected by the positive outcome.

Response 4.4: **Insight**
Listening and hearing lead to insight. The opportunity to truly decipher what the consumer is asking, wanting for, or looking for is paramount.

Response 4.5: **Empathy**
The general interest and then the ability take on the burden of the client.

Response 4.6: **Process**
Having the systems, protocols. and preparation in place to own the moment.

Response 4.7: **Adaptation**
The ability to adapt and conform to any kind of person, place, or ecosystem where opportunities arise. The ability to improvise and go off script.

Response 4.8: **Validation**
Helping clients and consumers know that you understand their wants, needs, and desires, and that these wants are warranted and important.

(*continued*)

(*Continued*)

Response 4.9: **Anticipation**

The preparation and the ability to see opportunities and issues before they arise.

Response 4.10: **Recovery**

Take responsibility and never be afraid to apologize. Its cliché but the customer is always right! Sometimes issues turn into the greatest Experiences.

Response 4.1:
Detail

To create something exceptional, your mindset must be relentlessly focused on the smallest detail.

—Hans Selye

One of the most powerful yet difficult precepts to get employees to adopt is the concept of attention to detail. It is that element of excess that puts the finishing touches on excellence. Disney boasts a world-famous level of attention to detail. It is one of the key factors that helps distinguish it from other organizations, and it hinges completely on the level of personal pride that employees take. Their willingness to go the extra mile makes the ultimate difference. Detail will manifest itself in many small ways, but it is often the most minute details that help make an Experience Exceptional.

What follow are several examples of visionary detail that many companies would think excessive and irrelevant, but those who strive for excellence in the Experience thought them to be a necessity.

An Angel

The Italian Pavilion at Epcot Center houses a replica of the famous bell tower at St. Mark's Campanile in Venice, Italy. Although the version at Epcot is only 83 feet tall, one-fourth the original, it is still impressive. The figure on top of the tower in Epcot is a full-size statue of an angel, painted in 24-karat gold paint. The detail is so exact that she even has fingernails. It's not likely that many guests notice this specificity—yet it is a point of pride to the designers, the builders, and the cast of Epcot.

Bump the Lamp

When the animated movie *Who Framed Roger Rabbit?* came out in 1988, it was another breakthrough for the Disney family. It was much more elaborate than *Mary Poppins* or *Pete's Dragon*; no computers were used to create any of the scenes, since they weren't sophisticated enough in the late 1980s. During the movie, Eddie takes Roger Rabbit to a back room in order to cut off his handcuffs. In the rush, Roger runs into a lamp that is suspended from the ceiling, but, in the early renderings, the shadows did not move as they normally would with a swinging lamp. The artists studied how a swinging lamp would cast a shadow and decided to redo the frames to incorporate the realistic shadow movement into the film. That extra attention to detail was called "bump the lamp." The principle is now used in Disney films, attractions, and shows in order to make them as detailed and realistic as possible.

Utility Pole

If you drive west on Interstate 4, outside of Celebration, Florida, in Kissimmee, you will see the most unusual utility pole in the world (at least in Disney World). The 80-foot-tall high-voltage utility pole is a giant Mickey Mouse head. How's that for getting your attention? Although it's not subtle, it exhibits the kind of attention to detail that most companies wouldn't even think about—and certainly wouldn't go to the tremendous expense just to make happen. That is the difference between great companies and average companies. Some merely see a pole; others see an opportunity to expand the Experience.

There are almost always at least four things in any company that, if significantly improved, could dramatically change the customer experience. It is often the attention to detail, the fine-tuning, and the "plussing" (as Disney calls it) that will help differentiate your company, your products, and your people from the competition. At Tractor Supply, it's the commitment to walking every customer to the desired product and making sure that every question is answered. At the Four Seasons Hotel, it's the commitment to taking notes on visitors so future stays will be more experiential. At Bethel World Outreach Church in Nashville, Tennessee, it's the practice of walking people to their pews in a style reminiscent of a wedding. The role of Response in this concept is to notice and accept when the opportunity arises—and then act on the opportunity to go the extra mile. While some individuals' natural reaction is to push off the responsibility or to ignore it, the appropriate response is to seize the moment and rise to the occasion.

Finding Tinker Bell

Some may ask: why the effort for the minute details of the Experience, especially if people do not always catch them? It is our belief, as it is the belief of the good people at Disney, that in a world where people are in a constant rush and often do not have time to soak up every aspect of your Experience, you had better find ways to wow them. *The National Center for Biotechnology Information tells us that the average human's attention span is only 8 seconds.* If 8 seconds is all the time that you have to make an Impression and to leave an indelible imprint on the mind, you had better do something that will cause a cerebral Connection with the customer on a level that is well outside of the realm of the ordinary.

We were recently touring Disney World in Orlando and our guide was showing us a few of the tiny details that are a part of the magic of Disney. After we took a ride on the Big Thunder Mountain Railroad, he pointed out a sliver, a small cutout, of one of the man-made rocks just outside of the ride. There she was—it was Tinker Bell! She was there as clear as day. The way that the sun cast the shadow was fantasy in its purest Walt Disney form. We were so impressed with the attention to detail of the creation, we stopped a couple of seven-year-old girls who were walking by with their parents. We pointed the silhouette out to them, and their reactions alone were worth the trip. It was magical. You see, the ride was fun, but the story of finding Tinker Bell was something that we will talk about forever. Detail creates stories. Stories create Ambassadors.

Foundation for Excellence

No one should expect you to be perfect; none of us are. However, people do expect you to give your best. This usually requires that we take our time so that we do whatever we are doing right the first time. We double-check our work before it reaches our customer or boss. We ensure that we are accurate and fair and open to feedback. We remain teachable and open to suggestions on improvement.

Those attention to detail opportunities—no matter how tiny the detail—are the things that can differentiate us from the competition. Most people and companies seem to be satisfied with the status quo. How often do we hear a "that's good enough" or "it's fine" that too many settle for? The people and companies that make history never settle for "good enough." And they are usually those that are tenacious about their attention to detail.

Quotient Question

Is there a certain attention to detail found within the Experience, and is there a genuine interest in meeting every need of the customer?

Actionables

Your attention to detail is one of the essential elements that transform you from being Average to being Exceptional.

Try this

☞ Ask yourself or the team, "What is one thing can we can do or say that may even go unnoticed, but will dramatically differentiate our service from our competition's service?" Come up with a new one on a monthly basis, and you will find soon enough that, to the public, these hidden details become not so hidden.

Try this

☞ Once each month, make the commitment to improve one thing in your repertoire of tactics that support the Experience. Learn a better way to calm an angry customer, study behavioral science to better connect with people and their needs, or simply become an expert on a specific product or portion of your service model.

Try this

☞ Make a list of every responsibility your have in relation to the customer. Under each category, write down the specific actions needed to make this an Exceptional Experience for the customer, and then begin to implement them. This is a formula for exceptionalism in everything you do! If it is not intentional, it won't happen.

Response 4.2:
Engagement

Employee engagement is the art of engaging people in authentic connections to roles, performance, relationship, customers, and happiness to transform work into results.

—David Zinger

Employee engagement involves a genuine interest in solving problems and creating service that yields results and relational outcomes. Far too many employees come across as apathetic or disinterested. Most customers have become adept at reading employees and determining who is focused and who is out to lunch. Too many employees who feel the job is beneath them are willing to go through the motions and have checked out long before their shift is over.

Tough Luck

When speaking, I often share a personal story of my Experience with a certain national hotel chain (that will go unnamed here). I was left at the curb by the hotel's shuttle bus, and then, after walking a half mile to the property, sweating and upset, I entered the hotel and noticed a few of the bellhops snickering at me. Well, this did not sit well with me, so I went inside to complain to a manager. The manager asked me to wait for her at the front desk, and a few moments later, out of the corner of my eye, I saw the manager walking out of the back of the hotel with her purse over her shoulder. I of course followed her and asked where she was going. Her reply? "My shift is over and the next manager will be here shortly." I travel a minimum of 150 nights a year and am—rather, *was*—an elite member of this hotel chain's customer base. This is a perfect example of a Toxic Experience, and I will certainly never darken the door of one of the company's hotels again.

Enthusiasm

Two of the most important qualities any employee can possess are energy and enthusiasm. While Bruce was at Walt Disney World, he was responsible for training hundreds of cast members. One of his most important roles was to coach them on how to present spiels at various attractions, such as the Jungle Cruise, the Hall of Presidents, Space Ship Earth, the Land Boat Ride, and others. For some reason, many cast members became very rigid and reserved the moment they picked up a microphone, likely as a result of nervousness. Consequently, their spiels were often dull and boring—the opposite of what Disney trained and expected.

Do you believe and trust people who seem lethargic and apathetic? Absolutely not. Speaking with energy and enthusiasm presents you as someone who is confident—and confidence translates to trust. These qualities also enable you to interact with others more effectively.

Expressing genuine interest in customers creates the connection and the foundation of the relationship we are looking for. The problem is that most employees are not engaged in their work and with their customers. In our research we have determined that every employee fits into one of three categories: champions, not engaged, or combative.

Defining Level of Engagement

- **Champions** are employees who tend to love their job, care about customers, and believe in the company and the work they do.
- **Not engaged** employees are essentially going through the motions. They have lost their passion and purpose for the work they do. This is just a job to them.
- **Combative** employees tend to be frustrated and angry at work. Unlike their "not engaged" counterparts, Combative employees can be saboteurs and can undermine the success of their coworkers and the company at large.

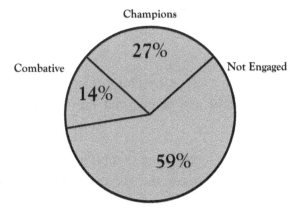

Source: Adapted from Gallup Management Journal, December 8, 2005.

According to research by the Gallup company (Gallup Management Journal, December 8, 2005), only 27 percent of employees are "Engaged," or as we call them, "Champions," 59 percent are "Disengaged" and a scary 14 percent are "Actively Disengaged" or as we refer to them, "Combative." This means that 73 percent of the employees in any organization are not fully engaged or vested in their jobs.

The good news is that the 27 percent who are actively engaged have all the opportunity to differentiate themselves from most of their coworkers. It is not a leader's job to get the combative employees involved. To the contrary, the leader should actively look to help them find another profession. The role of the leader is to make engagement part of the culture and to reach those employees who are not engaged. Engaged individuals tend to take a personal interest in others' needs and well-being. This idealism is the Response mindset and deals directly with the level of effort when there is an opportunity to serve to your fullest extent.

Quotient Question

Is there an emphasis on how to correctly and proactively respond to a customer's comment, desire, or complaint?

Actionables

It is better to respond to a need than to react. Responding is proactive, whereas reacting tends not to be strategic and rarely ends well.

Try this

☞ Create a responsive protocol list. Gather data on the issues that arise and be prepared with how to handle them.

Try this

☞ Make a mental note (not publicly) of who the champions, the disengaged, and the combative/Toxic employees are. Support and empower the champions, "coach up" and influence the disengaged, and remove the combative.

Try this

☞ When first meeting a customer, probe, ask questions, find the unmet want, and do whatever it takes to fill it. Develop a list of extra questions that can uncover the true need of the customer. Find the question behind the question (QBQ).

Response 4.3:
Urgency

Without a sense of urgency, desire loses its value.

—Jim Rohn

No one likes to wait—especially customers. Right or wrong, our society's sense of utility and pleasure is closely interwoven with that of efficiency and time. Most consumers are operating under a time crunch, even when they are supposed to be doing something fun, like going on vacation. When they have a hurry-up mentality, customers do not want to see employees who appear to be just on the clock, getting paid by the hour and not by how many customers they help. There must be a sense of urgency to the service you provide. When people sense that you don't care, the Experience is threatened. But when you take care of people with a sense of urgency, you have made them a priority and demonstrate that you feel they are important and that you value their time.

Urgency is a form of Response. It's not panic, rushing, or superficiality, but it means to be intentional, deliberate, and sensitive to the question, issue, or request. Whether you are paid a salary or an hourly wage, the frame of mind is in the appropriate Response to the customer. If you or your people happen to receive an hourly wage and you can adopt the right mindset and an appropriate sense of urgency, you'll realize that you are not actually paid by the hour. You are paid by the *value* you bring to that hour. It is entirely possible for two people to make $20 per hour doing essentially the same job, yet only one of them provides the value and efficiency of a $50 per hour employee. Simply stated, one person has discovered how to become more valuable in the work and that when you value the customer, you in turn become more valuable. The result is a better Experience for the customer and quite likely a pay raise or promotion for the employee.

Customers Are Your Priority

Urgency makes customers feel that they are your priority. When there is no fire or sense of urgency in what you do, you send the signal that their time—and ultimately they themselves—are not that important. As the expression goes, "Time is money." And while you can always get more money, you can never get more time. *According to Harrison Interactive, 75 percent of customers believe it takes too long to reach a live agent.* This is usually a process issue, but it still tells customers that they are not important. Our objective is to make every customer glad they chose to do business with us. It is easy to lose sight of this as a business owner, manager, or employee. We have so many things going on in our own lives and so many initiatives within our vocations that it's easy to lose sight of the organization's main priority and underlying goals.

In order to make customers feel like they are our priority, we actually must *make them our priority.* The key is first to listen to and then respond to their needs as quickly as possible. *Consider the following statistic: 72 percent of leaders do not return their phone calls and e-mails in a timely manner (within 24 hours), if at all.* We love the comment on most answering machines: "Your call is very important to us. Please

leave your name and phone number and I'll return your call right away."
How important is it truly if they never call back?!

We encounter indifferent Responses in every company and in every
industry. We have to be watchful to make sure that the rare occurrences
of a poor Response do not turn into general customer-facing apathy.
Just as you guard your margins and profits, so too should you guard
your urgency to serve your clients.

As we stated in the very beginning of the book, customers expect
two basic things: to be welcomed and to feel important. If you and your
company aren't doing an excellent job on those two things, you have a
major problem on your hands. Make customers your priority, exhibit a
sense of urgency, respond quickly, and genuinely care about the needs
of your customers. Each client request should become top of mind until
the consumer and client are not only satisfied, but cerebrally affected by
the positive outcome. The Experience as well as your revenues are at
stake.

Quotient Question

Is there a sense of urgency in helping or solving an issue for a
customer or client?

Actionables

Having a sense of urgency demonstrates to customers that you
value them and their time, which is priceless.

Try this

☞ Effective service requires insight on your part. Dig for the
   urgent concerns of customers, and then match your urgency
   with theirs. Practice this and see your customer satisfaction
   soar.

(continued)

(Continued)

Try this

☞ Be unique! Return all phone calls immediately if you are in a service role, within the hour if dealing with a client, and within 12 hours if you are traveling. You will amaze the customer or client on the other end of the line, and you will also demonstrate that you care and that you are a person of integrity.

Try this

☞ Incorporate listening exercises in your weekly or monthly meetings with coworkers. Focus on becoming an excellent listener, not just to what others say, but to the underlying thought or expectation. Actively listen; summarize and repeat information back to ensure you understand their intentions. Urgency is not just being intentional and moving fast. It is moving fast in the right direction.

Response 4.4:
Insight

A point of view can be a dangerous luxury when substituted for insight and understanding.

—Marshall McLuhan

Part of the art of customer care is effective listening and then truly hearing what customers want and need. We call it "listening to the voice of the customer." Disney uses multiple sources to hear what guests are saying—from exit questionnaires to mail-outs to marketing surveys. The more you know what your customers want, need, and expect, the better equipped you are to meet those needs. At the Magic Kingdom, City Hall is the central clearinghouse for complaints and comments by our guests. Of course, the first step to insight is actually wanting, actively seeking, and valuing the feedback—and of course, acting upon it.

> *You see, only one in 26 upset customers will take the time to tell you. But rest assured all of them will tell their friends and family. Therefore, a person who takes the time to write a letter of complaint or a note of endorsement virtually represents 26 people who have a similar viewpoint.*

Do you remember the Motel "X" story we shared at the beginning of the book? Organizations forget far too often that we live in a day and age when people rely on instant messaging, e-mail, and social media for the lion's share of their correspondence. *You see, only one in 26 upset customers will take the time to tell you.*

But rest assured all of them will tell their friends and family. Therefore, a person who takes the time to write a letter of complaint or a note of endorsement virtually represents 26 people who have a similar viewpoint. Bruce has shared his Motel "X" story with literally 160,000 people, many of whom will share that story with their friends. We always chuckle when we hear the words, "Well, you're the *only* person who has complained!" No, I'm the only person who has let you know of your problem. The others told all their friends; they just didn't tell you.

Knowledge or Understanding

Insight is power. Or better put, insight leads to knowledge, and knowledge is empowering. Using the knowledge that we gain is clearly the requirement; it's not enough to merely know something about someone. There are several ways to gain further insight as to what a client needs or is in search of, such as reading the customer's body language, expressions, and tone of voice. If you truly care, the person will tell you his or her state of mind at the time of engagement. The best customer service Ambassadors in the marketplace learn how to take on the mind of the customer. People walk around with little billboards on their foreheads that will tell you how they are feeling and what is wrong—or even right—with them. When a customer is confused, upset, lost, or even excited, we should be ready to respond accordingly. A heightened sense of awareness for the care of our customers, combined with the dedication and interest to ask the extra question to gain more insight, is one of the true secrets of executing an Exceptional Experience.

Quotient Question

How informed are employees with regard to the quality of the Experience they are providing, and are they consistently using the feedback to improve?

Actionables

Most of us have the gift of sight, but those who truly see are those who have insight and the ability to discern what others can't.

Try this

☞ At least once a day, identified employees need to ask customers the following questions: "How are we doing?" and "How can we get better?" Write down the comments, and keep a file on specific ways to improve your service.

Try this

☞ Before a customer leaves your area, say, "Is there anything else I can do for you?" Or perhaps, "Was there anything that we could have done to make this a more enjoyable Experience?"

Try this

☞ Make it a goal to gain new insight each week that will help you know what your customers expect. Be a student of customer feedback data and statistics on customer satisfaction. This information should be made available to every employee on a regular basis.

Response 4.5:
Empathy

I think we all have empathy. We may not have enough courage to display it.

—Maya Angelou

Empathy with our customers is one of the most important qualities we can develop. To feel what they feel—or at least to try to put ourselves in their situation or face their dilemma—is paramount to servicing them. Empathy is the ability to relate to others' thoughts, emotions, or experiences. Though it's often compared to sympathy—that is, the ability to understand and support others with compassion or sensitivity—it is actually more than that. Empathy requires the ability to step into someone else's shoes, be aware of that person's feelings, and understand his or her needs.

Exhibiting empathy in the workplace shows a deep respect for coworkers. It is a sign that you care, as opposed to employees who only follow the rules and regulations. An empathetic style of leadership has the power to make everyone feel part of the team, which in turn will increase productivity, morale, and loyalty. Empathy is a powerful tool in the personal arsenal of a well-liked and respected person. We could all take a lesson from nurses about being empathetic. Time and time again, nurses rate as the most trusted professionals, because they are able to display empathy and compassion in their daily roles and tasks. Most of them are able to do this because they truly care. This is why the nursing profession as a whole is often referred to as a calling, and not merely a job.

Stop Loss

We have a friend who recently took his six-year-old daughter to Disney World. The little girl spent three days acquiring as many autographs as possible and was riding the Jungle Cruise when she accidentally dropped her autograph book into the river. The book was not retrievable, and she was quite distraught over the incident. Upon seeing the tears of the little girl, one of the cast members (who actually had a daughter of her own) immediately asked the family what the problem was. After hearing the story, the cast member called for a supervisor. After explaining the case to the supervisor, the cast member was approved to accompany the family around the park and to the front of every line, where the autographs were recaptured for the little girl.

People lose things every day. There are also hundreds of children at every park, every day, crying for one reason or another. The difference here was the ability of a frontline cast member who saw the opportunity to empathize with a family, fix a problem, and save a vacation. That day, the family was successfully converted to Ambassadors for Disney. They share this story with everyone and with such a high level of emotion, you know that the empathetic actions of the Jungle Cruise cast member will never be forgotten.

Empathy and Likability Connection

People like other people who can relate to them. *More than 70 percent of the buying experience is based on the way customers perceived they were treated and how it made them feel.* Relating does not necessarily

More than 70 percent of the buying experience is based on the way customers perceived they were treated and how it made them feel.

mean that you are like them or have the same background, culture, or education. It simply implies an ability to see the world through others' eyes and to make them feel important. The Response Principle includes empathy as a needed ingredient to be able to serve with precision. If you cannot understand and connect to customers' needs, there is no way you'll be able to help them. From what we've seen, the reason people do so well at Disney World is the likability factor. The individuals who shine there and in the marketplace in general are those who possess empathetic qualities and abilities.

Quotient Question

Is it clear that the employees care, and is it the desire of the employees to truly understand the wants and needs of the customer?

Actionables

Being able to relate and truly empathize with the needs of customers creates trust and connects with them on a personal level.

Try this

☞ Even though it is difficult to empathize or feel what someone is going through, you can still connect. Use relational exchanges such as this one to empathize with the customer: Please help me understand how we can best take care of this for you.

Try this

☞ Make a list of the top 10 behaviors you can enhance or adopt that will help you develop Exceptional people skills. The core of empathy is being able to relate and communicate effectively.

(*continued*)

(*Continued*)

Try this

☞ In your weekly or monthly team meetings, practice mirroring your customers. When you are dealing with a difficult customer, mirroring him or her will help you empathize and connect. Match the person's voice pattern, volume, eye contact, even style and choice of phrasing. People feel much more comfortable with people who are like them.

Response 4.6:
Process

Science is the process that takes us from confusion to understanding.

—Brian Greene

Excellence is not something you achieve once and can claim to be finished with; rather, it is a process. Disney could not exist without systems, protocols, and preparation. To this day, Disney remains unique in the way its employees work so *seamlessly* with each other, which of course does not happen by chance. The Disney secret to this success is a proprietary process. The preparation and effort that cast members put forth is staggering, and is one of the reasons why the Disney Experience is so synonymous with excellence. *According to a recent consumer survey report by Forrester, more than 50 percent of customers felt their issues or concerns were not resolved.* This is sometimes an issue of effort. However, more times than not, the issue is a lack of process that ensures that questions are always answered and issues are always taken care of.

> *According to a recent consumer survey report by Forrester, more than 50 percent of customers felt their issues or concerns were not resolved.*

Walt Disney World is made up of nearly 70,000 cast members who work in 1,500 different jobs—and who are all part of an elaborate process that works. Bruce had the privilege of starting off in the Entertainment division at Disneyland, and then moved to Florida to join the Entertainment division of Walt Disney World. When he was given the opportunity to create his own position, he became part of the Operations division—or as most people know it, Attractions. As he began to develop the cast in Attractions, Bruce discovered the need to improve service excellence, communication, teamwork, attitudes, and leadership development as well. He was able to witness firsthand the amount of emphasis that was placed on the Disney process. Soon Bruce was receiving calls from the Merchandise, Foods, Security, Parking, Housekeeping, and Guest Relations divisions to assist each of them in improving their service process as well. The key for Bruce and the leadership at Disney was to realize that a process is not simply about checking boxes and protocols. Rather, it is a commitment to seamlessly integrating people into a planned Experience.

Cross-Educating

Although there were some rivalries between divisions at Disney, most seemed to work well and respect one another's territory. With an organization as large and complex as Disney World, it is essential that various departments, teams, and individuals work together for a common goal; otherwise, the show will fail. Bruce helped develop a process at Disney called "cross-educating." If there was a conflict between one department and another that needed to work together, two or three key individuals from one of the departments would be sent to attend a meeting with the other department. They would explain what their responsibility was in relation to facilitating the show and how they felt the other department could best assist them. Then, the process would be reversed and two or three key people from the other department would be sent to explain what they needed and how they felt the two departments could work together best. The point is to make sure that everyone has a voice in the process and that each voice is acknowledged and heard. Amazing Experiences are created through these kinds of processes and this type of communication.

Aligning Process with Vision

When there was an opening of a major show or event involving multiple divisions at Disney, Bruce's coworkers held meetings two, three, and even 12 months ahead of time in order to get everyone on board. However, sometimes our vision, innovation, or new idea can be quite difficult to impart to others whom we must count on to carry it out. To do so, we need to have a strategy and a process in place, and must connect them with the vision in every detail. Then the process and order of the actions that take place to fulfill the strategy must be executed in the spirit of the vision itself. No sophisticated organization's plan or Experience can survive for long without a vision, strategy, and process. Without the alignment of these items, it is impossible to have everyone on board and reading from the same page.

Quotient Question

Is there a clear process and a set of protocols for responding to customer and client needs?

Actionables

As an employee or leader of an organization, you are also an internal consultant. Constantly monitor, measure, and improve your internal processes. After all, "process makes perfect!"

Try this

☞ On a monthly basis, e-mail or provide a survey to loyal customers. Ask them specific questions: "Did you feel that we were efficient and organized?" "Was it easy to find everything?" "What would you change?" "What problems did you encounter within your Experience, and what would you like us to do to correct them?"

(continued)

(Continued)

Try this

☞ Identify a team or a department you are having difficulty connecting with. Invite two or three key people from that department to a future staff meeting to discuss ongoing issues between your departments and possible solutions. Then reverse it and send two or three of your people to their staff meeting. It will open doors and processes that seemed impossible before.

Try this

☞ Once each month in your meetings, site examples of what worked and what didn't. Identify an action plan for the next month to correct or eliminate the misses from the Experience, and build models and a process upon the hits!

Response 4.7:
Adaptation

The measure of intelligence is the ability to change.

—Albert Einstein

Excellent companies and the excellent people who work in them are able to adapt to changing times. In the twentieth century, the Swiss were known as the watch experts. If you wanted a great watch, you would go to the Swiss. In fact, in the 1960s, there were 1,500 master watchmakers and designers in Switzerland. In the 1970s quartz crystal was discovered—a new crystal that would revolutionize the watch industry. The developers of the quartz crystal first introduced it to the Swiss; however, these renowned watchmakers did not readily embrace it. The Japanese, in contrast, fully welcomed and began utilizing quartz crystal. Consumer demands shifted toward the Japanese products, and as a result, the Swiss employment in the watch industry dropped from 90,000 in 1970 to just 28,000 in 1988. You can count on change happening in your day, in your products, in your industry, and within your customers' Experience. Your ability to identify change and adopt or adapt could very well write the script for your organization's future.

The Only Constant

There is only one constant in business: change. Bruce has a friend who used to sell nine-foot satellite dishes to residential and commercial customers. He had done quite well for years and decided to purchase a large quantity toward the end of the year at a discount. Shortly after he filled a small warehouse with the large dishes, the market was flooded with the much smaller and much less expensive three-foot satellite dishes. Almost overnight, he couldn't give his older, obsolete satellite dishes away and he was forced to declare bankruptcy.

Walt Disney World opened in July 1971. At that time, Tomorrowland was state of the art and beautiful. Fast-forward 40 years, those attractions are no longer state of the art; in fact, they look dated. One such attraction was the "Carousel of Progress." It was originally designed for the 1964 World's Fair, but probably hadn't been updated much since then. Management had the same concerns for Epcot, which opened in 1982. One of Walt's key principles when he introduced the concept of Walt Disney World and Epcot to the world in 1966 was: "It will always be in a state of becoming. It will be a living blueprint for the future." However, sometimes even Disney can be slow to change.

Why Change?

Change comes easily for some of us but is like pulling teeth for the rest of us. There is an expression in business today: "Adapt or die." Walt Disney loved change. He once said, "I don't like to repeat successes. I like to go on to other things." But what about those of us who are averse to change and who feel comfortable with the status quo? Derrick Johnson, creator of the "Voices of Liberty" at Epcot, once told Bruce, "If you ever have the opportunity to do something new as opposed to something you've done before, always take the new thing. You can always go back to the thing you've done before if you fail." Life is designed to involve stretching, growing, and challenging yourself to be better, to improve, and to be different. Variety itself often builds self-confidence unlike anything else.

Comedian Robin Williams passed away while we were in the process of writing this book. We have always been fans of Robin because of his creative mind, but especially his off-the-wall, adventurous spirit. Here was someone who got nervous each time before he entertained, and yet knew that the rewards were just one step beyond being nervous. Robin was a comedic genius. His willingness to adapt and enlarge his capacity led him from local clubs to the grandest of all stages and eventually to the Academy Award podium. Robin Williams definitely knew how to harness the power of adaptation.

Adapting to Customers

Along with innovation and adapting to the changing environment around your organization, adjusting to meet your customers' immediate and long-term needs is pivotal to the Experience. The ability to conform to any kind of person, place, or ecosystem is a point of inference that must stay top of mind with leadership and employees alike. *In a study administered by Marketing Metrics, it was discovered that 60 percent of repeat customers remained loyal due to the ability of the organization to evolve and adapt to their needs.* We have to have the ability and the expertise to improve on the Experience and, when appropriate, go off script. But to be empowered to do this, you must first be equipped. Adaptation says I. C.A.R.E.!

A great example of this is the employee empowerment model that most Four Seasons properties have adopted. Employees are empowered to solve problems and even spend a discretionary amount of money to resolve an issue for a customer or client. While you certainly would not do this for just any employee, the employees who are granted decision making power at a Four Seasons are pros. They have been trained, prepared, and equipped to have appropriate Responses and exact actions that are congruent with an Exceptional Experience and a proprietary process.

The Shirt off Their Back

As discussed before, sometimes you need to adapt in a consumer's moment of crisis. I recently traveled to Atlanta with my wife Kimberly. I was flying in for a business meeting, and the airline lost my baggage. We expected that the airline would be able to deliver the baggage in time for me to change, but I received a call from the airline about an hour before the meeting stating that my clothes would not be making it to me at the hotel any time soon. We were staying at the Intercontinental Buckhead in Atlanta and I was wearing jeans, a T-shirt, and sandals—not entirely appropriate wear for a professional meeting.

So I went to one of the bellmen, who remembered me from my previous visits, and we walked together to the front desk. The gentleman asked for the hotel manager. The bellman told the manager the issue, and I felt an immediate sense of peace when the manager turned to me and said, "This is no problem, sir."

The manager immediately took me into the inner sanctum of the Intercontinental Buckhead and they found me a uniform that fit. These gray, pinstriped suits are nicer than anything I own. The manager winked at me and said, "For the next three hours, you can be one of us. Just do not forget to bring back the suit." He then took me to the gift shop where we found a shirt, and then they handed me three ties to go upstairs to see which one I wanted to purchase. I made it to the meeting on time, and the people actually commented on how nice I looked. What an Experience!

In concocting the Exceptional, a person or a team must have the ability to adapt and respond. Not only should the team in Atlanta feel good that they were the positive variable in one man's crisis; they should be proud that they've earned a client for life.

Quotient Question

Do the employees possess the ability to adapt to change, and are they empowered to respond correctly when any opportunity to help arises?

Actionables

All forward-thinking experts are change artists. The inability to change and adapt will constrict future progress, growth, and advancement.

Try this

☞ The next time you are faced with an issue that is outside the realm of your training or processes, stay calm and focus on what the best possible outcome would be for the customer. Then make sure that you document the issue and communicate this to the organization, department, or team so a protocol or process can be derived.

Try this

☞ Adopt this simple five-part process that internally can help with adapting to change:

1. Recognize that change happens.

2. Create a game plan and process for adaptation.

3. Gradually integrate change into your environment.

4. Discuss the change with others: how did they adapt, and why it is beneficial?

5. Focus on positive attitudes and actions.

(continued)

(*Continued*)

Try this

☞ The next time you are confronted with unexpected change or perhaps a fork in the road with regard to your Experience offering, make a T chart with the pros and cons and the outcomes of each. If the outcomes and potentials for success are greater than the cons, determine to move full speed ahead with the change.

Response 4.8:
Validation

The deepest principle of human nature is the craving to be appreciated.
—William James

On the 20th anniversary of her television show, Oprah Winfrey made a remarkable statement. She said, "I've interviewed thousands of people from all walks of life over the past 20 years, from paupers who have nothing to billionaires who have everything and everyone in between, but I've discovered that there is a common thread running through each of these people. They all want to be validated." No matter where you go in life, the levels of success you have achieved, or the name you have made for yourself, you still need to feel you have value.

Recently, Bruce received a call from his sister-in-law, who was very upset with a hospital. Her sister had had an apparent stroke the day before, so she was rushed to the emergency department of a local women's hospital. Her sister is not married, and Bruce's sister-in-law did not have a power of attorney to answer on her behalf, so no one would provide his sister-in-law with any information. The medical staff kept asking her sister the same questions over and over; yet she couldn't answer due to her condition.

Bruce's sister experienced the "three D's" from the entire staff: disconnected, disengaged, and disinterested. She was amazed at how rude, abrupt, and uncaring people could be when the very people they were paid to help were scared, confused, and frustrated.

Every person wants to sense that they are important and valued—to know that the choices they make are good, and if they are not, to know why. In this way, they need their opinions and their time to be validated as well. *A recent study by the Aberdeen Group stated that 70 percent of best-in-class customer experience experts use customer feedback to make strategic decisions.* If we do not know how they feel and what they want, how can we know how best to serve them? Validation should be present in every response, whether in defining organizational strategy or with regard to direct customer interactions. When you validate someone, you convey that you care.

> *A recent study by the Aberdeen Group stated that 70 percent of best-in-class customer experience experts use customer feedback to make strategic decisions.*

Do the Right Thing

Most people aren't looking for special consideration or the star treatment; however, they *do* want to be treated fairly and with respect. High-end department store Nordstrom has a very simple yet effective philosophy: "Do the right thing." In other words, if it is best for customers and works in *their* favor, then do it. It doesn't get much simpler than that.

An elderly woman went into chain restaurant Dave's BBQ and bought lunch. Since she couldn't finish it all, she took it home and put it in her refrigerator for more than a week, then fed it to her dog. The dog proceeded to get sick, and the lady returned to Dave's to complain. After hearing her story, the manager asked her how much she paid for the lunch and cheerfully refunded her money.

One of the employees was incredulous and asked the manager why he had refunded her money when it was clearly the lady's own fault. The manager said, "I would much rather compensate her for an eight-dollar meal than to risk losing her business—and all her friends'—forever."

Carl Sewell, owner of Sewell Village Cadillac in Dallas, Texas, estimates that the value of a lifelong customer is $322,000. He said, "It doesn't make a lot of sense to argue about a $50 part when you stand to lose $322,000." If you will treat people fairly, give them the benefit of the doubt, and make them feel important and valued, you will not only have a customer for life; you will have the opportunity to convert them to Ambassadors who will share their Experience with others.

Quotient Question

Does the organization make the effort to understand the customer's wants, needs, and desires and acknowledge to its customers that they are indeed important?

Actionables

It is very important to help your clients or consumers understand that you acknowledge their wants, needs, and desires as being warranted and important.

Try this

☞ Whenever customers offer a suggestion, criticism, or compliment, sincerely thank them for their comment and make a validating statement, such as, "That is an excellent point. Let me see how we can apply that to our service. Thank you."

Try this

☞ Create a profile of how your clients and customers like to be treated. Then make this profile the foundation of the Experience. Put yourself in their shoes. Then ask yourself, "What do I need to change in order to provide that person with an Exceptional Experience?"

(continued)

(Continued)

Try this

☞ Each time you are able to improve, or you witness someone executing the Exceptional, even if it is a small baby step, you need to celebrate and encourage the team and your coworkers. Those incremental steps are the building blocks to consistency and excellence, so celebrate the minute accomplishments as well as the major achievements.

Response 4.9:
Anticipation

Wisdom consists of the anticipation of consequences.

—Norman Cousins

In most cases, we know what customers want and need. The challenge comes in how well we're able to anticipate and deliver on what customers want and need. Excellent companies and excellent employees are focused on delivering not just "good" or "strong," but Exceptional. Wayne Gretzky is famous for saying, "I skate to where the puck is gonna be, not where it has been." The people who truly make a name for themselves in the service business are able to *anticipate* what the customer wants and then deliver it. And the truly great ones deliver services and items that customers don't yet know that they want and need. Who would expect that, upon going in for a major surgery, your nerves would be calmed significantly if you have the feeling that you are checking into a deluxe hotel? The Mayo Clinic did this!

Illustrious hotels such as the Ritz-Carlton and the Four Seasons create systems that track past preferences of their guests. One guest preferred Pepsi over Coke products. Even though the hotel served only Coke, the manager made a special effort to have a six-pack of ice-cold Pepsi waiting in the guest's room when he arrived. Another guest liked a certain kind of pillow that the manager special-ordered and kept specifically for that guest. Those little touches and the ability to anticipate someone's needs well in advance will set you apart from others. People do not remember the big things nearly to the degree that they remember the little things. Whether the customer spends a fortune or a small amount with your business is irrelevant, as either way, they share their Experience with others. The little things we do count the most in service.

Disney Awareness

Disney is famous for anticipating guest needs *before* they arise. One of the ways that the cast members are able to set themselves apart is by having the heightened sense of awareness needed to see the unseen before it gets seen! If you know what the majority of issues will be in a restaurant, on the parade route, within an attraction, or with the guest flow in a shop, and you are able to alleviate those issues in advance, the customer's Experience is never negatively affected. Oftentimes, the guest may not even have known there would have been a problem. At Disney, the awareness objective is always to eliminate any problem or glitch before it is noticed.

Know Your Purpose

In order to properly anticipate the actions needed for the delivery of an Exceptional Experience, all employees need to know what their purpose is—in other words, why they do what they do. Any person in your organization should be able to walk up to any other person and ask: "How does what you do *directly* or *indirectly* impact the customer Experience?" If they can't answer this basic question, then you have a leadership problem or a communication issue. *Unfortunately, in our internal polling, only 29 percent of the employees knew what their primary purpose (true role) in the organization was.*

> *Unfortunately, in our internal polling, only 29 percent of the employees knew what their primary purpose (true role) in the organization was.*

Employees must all be constantly aware of how their job, their attitude, their performance, and customer satisfaction are directly linked—and must appreciate why that is important. When you recognize that your purpose is taking care of the customer, then everything else you do becomes abundantly clear.

Quotient Question

Do the employees of the organization know their purpose in the delivery of the Experience, and are they equipped to anticipate problems and solutions as issues occur?

Actionables

Success is often contingent upon expecting excellence, anticipating how to overcome obstacles, and delivering on those expectations.

Try this

☞ Always communicate with your customers; let them know what to expect, and be honest and direct. Apply the UPOD concept: underpromise, overdeliver. Set their expectations one step lower in order to deliver more than promised—more than expected.

Try this

☞ Make a Connection to the profiles of your clients and customers and their preferences, and then anticipate what will make their Experience Exceptional. Always remember "onstage." Being intentional in your attention to each and every "guest" will allow you to maximize your role and to deliver your best every time you are in the presence of a customer.

(continued)

(Continued)

Try this

☞ Make a list (that will become a checklist) of every aspect of the job or role you play and how it directly or indirectly impacts the customer. Next, identify what you need to do in order to take your "Experience game" to the next level.

Response 4.10:
Recovery

There are no secrets to success. It is the result of preparation, hard work, and learning from failure.

—Colin Powell

Billy Riggs is a friend of Bruce's and a world-class magician. He was invited to perform at the Atlantis Resort on Paradise Island in the Bahamas. He decided to take his wife and baby son with him, but they missed their connection in Miami and arrived after midnight at the Atlantis resort. They were exhausted, and he had all of his business and magic equipment, along with their personal gear, stroller, and the baby. He filled two full carts with luggage and gear. The clerk gave them their key and the bellman pushed one cart with Billy pushing the other on the 10-minute walk to their room.

After taking the elevator to their floor, they finally opened the door to their room, only to be met by the screams of a woman inside. Billy quickly closed the door, and trekked 10 minutes back to the front desk. This scenario went on two additional times with occupied rooms. At 2:30 a.m., they went back to the front desk after the third incident and a manager stepped in to resolve the issue.

The manager apologized and said, "We're going to upgrade your room." He then took them on yet another 10-minute walk to the elevator. The bellman pushed the button to the top floor, and when the double doors opened, they heard what sounded like angels singing accompanied by a grand piano, and saw huge floor-to-ceiling windows overlooking the Caribbean.

When Billy tells people about his family's stay in the Atlantis, they don't recall the multiple room screw-ups or repeated trips to and from the front desk in the wee hours of the morning. Rather, they recount details about the hotel's phenomenal recovery and the incredible time his family spent in the penthouse.

Service recovery is imperative. Customers know and understand that things go wrong. Most people are not unreasonable; however, they detest when employees sweep slipups under the carpet, when they constantly make excuses, or *especially* when they blame others for a problem. Customers generally don't care whose fault a particular misstep is; they just want to know who is going to fix it, and how. Excellent people and Exceptional companies have a system and a process of what to do when the Experience takes a turn for the worse.

According to NLM Consulting, roughly 96 percent of unhappy customers never complain to brands or service providers; however, they do tell their friends. They have also discovered that if you are able to resolve a problem, between 54 percent and 70 percent will return and give you a second chance. If you do not resolve it, 46 percent will never do business with you again.

The Bottom Line

There is a three-ton granite rock sitting outside Stew Leonard's, a very successful grocery store in Norwalk, Connecticut. Engraved on the rock are two rules that you've likely seen at other stores:

Rule #1: "The customer is always right."

Rule #2: "If the customer is ever wrong, re-read Rule #1."

Although it may be old and trite and a cliché, it is true: "The customer is always right." When things go wrong, which they are prone to do, your primary responsibility is to fix them ASAP or immediately—whichever comes first.

Reversal of Fortune

When Bruce was a Fantasyland supervisor in the Magic Kingdom, he received a call to come to the Dumbo ride immediately. Upon arriving, he found that two dads had been jostling for their place in line and one of them hauled off and hit the other dad. Rather than kick the aggressor out of the park, he pulled him and his son into Pinocchio's Village Haus (a fast-food restaurant) and said, "Look, I don't want to get Security involved because it will spoil your vacation. Why don't you and your son slip out the back and go to some other part of the park and forget this ever happened?" The father thanked Bruce and left.

However, when Bruce told the other dad what he had done, the man was livid and demanded that he press charges. So they filled out a complaint and had two undercover guards spend another hour and a half looking around the park for the alleged aggressor. Finally, they thought they spotted him at Big Thunder Mountain Railroad. Security escorted the man and his family up to the office and proceeded to interrogate him. After an hour, Security asked Bruce to come to identify him as the individual who had hit the other dad. The moment Bruce entered Security and saw the man and he said, "You've got the wrong guy!"

Now *Disney* was responsible—and it was Bruce's fault for trying to be a nice guy and *failing* to contact Security in the first place. In order to make up for his mistake, Bruce spent the next two hours getting the family of the wrongly accused man onto any ride they wanted with no waiting ("back dooring"), as well as arranging for special pictures with the characters, Cokes, and ice cream bars. They had a great time. Four weeks later, Bruce received a very nice letter from the mother, genuinely thanking him for saving their vacation. She wrote, "If it weren't for you, our vacation would have been a disaster. How can I thank you enough?" So, Bruce was both the culprit *and* the hero of the story.

We are all going to make mistakes. But it's the way we respond and then recover from them that customers will remember. The secret to an exceptional Experience is not the absence of imperfections but the relentless resolve to overcome them.

Quotient Question
Is there a commitment by the employees of the organization to recover the Experience when service or the interaction breaks down?

Actionables
We don't prove our worth to customers when things always go right as much as by our immediacy in resolving problems when they go wrong.

Try this
☞ Before any customer leaves, ask, "Were we able to take care of your needs today?" or "Is there anything else we can do to make this an even better Experience for you?" Be sincere,

(*continued*)

(Continued)

and customers are much more likely to give you feedback
that can improve you and your company today and in the
future.

Try this

☞ Whenever there is a problem, identify it, isolate it, and then
fix it. Take personal ownership and do your best to resolve it
in the first 10 minutes. Most problems are easiest to resolve
in the early stages before they begin to fester and frustrate
the customer.

Try this

☞ When a problem arises, use the L.E.A.R.N. system that
Bruce adopted at Disney.

L. ~ Listen: Listen closely to identify the problem.

E. ~ Empathize: Place yourself in the customer's shoes.

A. ~ Apologize: Take responsibility.

R. ~ Resolve: Work urgently but calmly to resolve the
issue.

N. ~ Normalize: Restore the customer to the previous state
prior to the issue.

Part III
Backstage (The Internal Interface)

Chapter Eight
Principle 5: Exceptionals

You can design and create, and build the most wonderful place in the world. But it takes people to make the dream a reality.

—Walt Disney

Synonyms for the word *exceptional* include *rare, extraordinary, excellent,* and *superior.* We can't possibly expect to live up to these powerful words even with an above-average effort or level of execution. The secret behind the Experience is the relational expertise and execution that come from the people who own and are in charge of its delivery. As we have already stated, we would summarize this book as a tool for creating Ambassadors of the Experience, and it is impossible to deliver an Exceptional Experience without internal Ambassadors. If the management team and employees are not prepared, empowered, and responsible for the Experience, creating and executing the Exceptional become an impossibility. The Experience must be internalized within the organization and its people.

Why Exceptional?

Exceptional service cannot occur without each individual, department, and organization collectively raising the bar to establish expectations of excellence. Our research uncovered a direct correlation between employee satisfaction and customer satisfaction. In virtually every category, Exceptional employees (and Exceptional companies) that are happier and more fulfilled provide much better service, and are far more adept at satisfying customers.

As at Disney, the Experience begins "backstage." The way that you treat your partners and your fellow employees will ultimately correlate to the way that those colleagues treat and interact with your customers in your absence. We have five underlying I. C.A.R.E. Principles (Impression, Connection, Attitude, Response, and Exceptionals) and more than 50 specific points of inference relating to those Principles in this book. And while we present the Exceptionals last, they are truly the foundation to creating the Exceptional Experience.

Our research tells us that less than 3 percent of American organizations are executing the Experience at an Exceptional level.

Our research tells us that less than 3 percent of American organizations are executing the Experience at an Exceptional level. Where are you? This section is about the Experience internally as it is being incubated for external use. If you get nothing else from this project, focus on these precepts and watch the client interface in your organization take shape and become something that you can be proud of—and something your customers will begin to share with others.

Exceptionals: Ten Disney-Inspired Non-Negotiables

Exceptionals 5.1: Culture

You perfect your culture through a system of breathing the internal Experience into the lives of those who carry the external Experience to others.

Exceptionals 5.2: Excellence

Excellence is the relentless pursuit of perfection despite understanding that true perfection is not achievable.

Exceptionals 5.3: Ethos

This is the *why* behind the people, product, and service that the Experience is supporting.

Exceptionals 5.4: Accountability

This requires committing to an agreed-upon level of execution and delivery of the Experience.

Exceptionals 5.5: Teaming

This element states that the Experience is equal to the sum of its parts and people.

Exceptionals 5.6: Investment

This is the amount of effort, development, love, and encouragement given to the employees—and anyone else responsible for delivering the Experience.

Exceptionals 5.7: Training

The internal Ambassadors of the Experience must be prepared.

Exceptionals 5.8: Development

Apprenticeship has always been the secret to duplication of talent. If your Experience is to be a repeatable one, discipleship and development are a must.

(continued)

(*Continued*)

Exceptionals 5.9: **Extraordinary**

This is the tenacity to fight the thought of Average and the will to see your team members execute the Experience with perfection.

Exceptionals 5.10: **Enjoyment**

The magic happens when the employees and Ambassadors are having the same level of enjoyment as the customers. The power of a positive atmosphere can never be underestimated!

Exceptionals 5.1:
Culture

You have to maintain a culture of transformation to stay true to your values.

—Jeff Weiner

Culture is king. You must create, develop, and protect your culture by consistently breathing the organization's values into the lives of those who carry the deliverables and the brand message. Though none of the precepts that we discuss in this book are really up for negotiation, this one is an *absolute Non-Negotiable*. Culture is the lifeblood of the organization and something that you must develop, teach, and preserve at all costs.

Culture of Excellence

The key to creating a culture of excellence is to establish standards that do not deviate. It all starts with a vision of where you and your company plan to be in the next five to ten years. Changing culture is not a quick fix; rather, it is a process you will have to model and develop over time. *The statistics are jarring: in an independent study we conducted, we found that roughly 70 percent of all employees in any organization*

The statistics are jarring: in an independent study we conducted, we found that roughly 70 percent of all employees in any organization are average performers, another 15 percent are excellent, and the final 15 percent are poor.

are average performers, another 15 percent are excellent, and the final 15 percent are poor. The key to changing culture is to eliminate the poor performers while raising as many average performers to the excellent category as possible. This is the responsibility of leadership.

We describe the creation and further development of culture as a *path*. The first step to creating a culture of excellence is to determine *who* should be on the path; and the second is determining who needs to be on *another path*. One reason Disney is so effective is the fact that the leaders have become experts at distinguishing between these two, and then deciphering what role people should play on that path.

Core Values

The precursor to excellence in any organization must be the core values. Since the start of Disneyland and continuing with subsequent openings of each of the other Disney parks, there have been four values that have shaped everything the brand does and that broadcast the corporate values throughout the organization.

Dick Nunis and Van France created the four core standards prior to the opening of Disneyland in 1955, and they have remained part of the Disney philosophy for the past 60 years. These four standards were Safety, Show, Courtesy, and Capacity. Though they have been modified slightly in recent years (Capacity later evolved to Efficiency), they reflect the consistency and importance of who Disney people are and what they stand for. They are the core priorities that virtually every decision and every action stem from with a Disney park. The current standards are:

1. **Safety:** Every precaution is taken to ensure that each guest is safe during the Experience.
2. **Courtesy:** Every guest is treated with respect and as a valued VIP.

3. **Show:** Every aspect of the Disney show and cast members must be excellent.

4. **Efficiency:** Every guest Experience must run smoothly and seem effortless.

Safety

Without Safety, nothing else matters. Disney can serve the best food, give your kids an hour of private time with the characters, put on shows, and provide spectacular rides—but if you slip and break your ankle because a cast member was careless and didn't clean up a mess, your trip is ruined. Nothing is more important than guest safety and your customers' well-being.

Courtesy

As mentioned earlier, the two top attributes that every customer wants from a company are friendly employees and feeling welcome and important. Courtesy is the foundation of respect. Without the fundamentals of friendliness, kindness, being personable, and taking a genuine interest in others, you aren't showing the basic respect that every customer expects, needs, and deserves.

Show

As we've emphasized throughout the book, Disney is one big, well-planned, and highly choreographed show. Not everyone likes the same style of music, performances, rides, food, or anything else, though; so Disney offers a variety of shows within the show. But regardless of the music, performances, rides, or food, it is all about delivering excellence at every juncture. Regardless of where you work and what you do, you must deliver your offering with excellence. Otherwise, it isn't worth your time and the customer's money.

Efficiency

Customers hate waiting in line, sitting on hold, or being delayed. In general, people are impatient. Especially nowadays, we want fast food, instant potatoes, quick car lubes, drive-through banking, TV dinners, and anything else that saves time. This is why Disney trains each cast member to do two basic things: touch (engage) with each guest to let all guests know that they are important, and expedite them through the process as quickly as possible. When there are 40,000 guests who visit a Disney park in a day, cast members strive to be three things: excellent, effective, and efficient.

In order for your company to succeed and for each employee to be focused, it is imperative to establish standards that become the priorities of importance. Everything you do in business and for your customer must be filtered through your standards. Even though the show may be important, it never supersedes courtesy—and nothing supersedes safety. There must always be a reason why you do what you do.

Traditions

From our perspective, the very first day of your employment is the most important. This is what sets the tone and establishes much of the rest of your career with the company. At Walt Disney World, your first day is your orientation or, as Disney calls it, Traditions. Traditions is aptly named, as it establishes and ingrains the traditions of Disney's past, present, and future into each new cast member.

After employees are "cast" in a "role" in Walt Disney World, they must attend a multiday introduction to Disney and have a thorough overview of Disney's heritage before they are released to their ultimate work areas. For cast members to be successful, they must understand their role in the show in order to learn how they best represent the Disney way of serving guests.

There are more than 1,500 different job categories within Walt Disney World. Every cast member is "auditioned" (or hired) to fit the "role" and to model the attitudes, behaviors, and expectations of what Disney excellence is. The standards and expectations for the Disney cast are fairly high and demanding. It's difficult to smile when it's 95 degrees out and humidity is 90 percent, but this feat becomes possible when it is not just part of the job, but also part of the culture.

Quotient Question

Is the culture perfected through a system of breathing the internal Experience into the lives of those who carry the external Experience to others?

Actionables

Virtually everything we do emanates from the culture of who we are and what we stand for.

Try this

☞ Write down a list of the qualities that you feel best define your company. Then, once a month, survey two customers, one who is a regular and one who is new, to see if both customers can see qualities similar to the ones you defined. If not, you now have an action plan to reinstitute.

Try this

☞ Identify four values similar to Disney's Safety, Courtesy, Show, and Efficiency that reflect the values of your company. On a scale of 1 to 10, evaluate how effectively your company and you personally are measuring up to each value. Next, design an action plan on the steps necessary to improve.

(continued)

(Continued)

Try this

☞ In your company archives, research the documents and principles that served as the foundation of your company and its history. Create a board with copies of original pictures, quotes, and captions defining the traditions of your company, and place it in an area accessible to staff. Once a month, ask yourself and the team, "How do we retain the principles and character that made us or is making us great?"

Exceptionals 5.2:
Excellence

Excellence is not a skill. It is an attitude!

—Ralph Marston

Excellence is not about being perfect or demanding perfection of others; we all know that this simply isn't possible. Rather, excellence is about striving to get better on a daily basis. The pursuit is contagious in an organization and is one of the catalysts of great culture. It is the *pursuit* of perfection while having the wisdom and grace to understand that is it unachievable.

Much of Disney's magic lies in its image and reputation. The Disney theme parks enjoy a very positive worldwide reputation, and Disney leadership has worked very hard to create a brand and image of excellence. However, it wasn't always that way. Many of the cast members who were present for Disneyland's original opening back in 1955 referred to that day as "Black Sunday." Many of the rides did not work. There were supposed to be a select number of guests and dignitaries at the opening, but instead people printed fake tickets and what was slated to be a few thousand visitors turned into 28,000 and overwhelmed the park. The Disney difference is not that they do not have problems; it's that they learn from them. Bruce often likes to say, "Perfection is impossible, but somewhere in between our current state and our grasp for perfection, we *can* reach the point of excellence."

The Pressure of Excellence

One of the problems that Disney and other Exceptional organizations often face is falling victim to their own excellence. When you are very good at something—and you manage your customers' expectations to one of excellence—the bar is often set too high to repeatedly *exceed* those expectations. When guests visit a Disney park once every three or five years, they tend to remember the best of the best—even if not every moment of the Experience was magical.

Let's assign a number to a previous customer experience you had, and let's say you gave it an 8 on a scale of 1 to 10. You went to Disney, had a good trip, and you mentally rated it an 8. It's been five years since your last visit and the anticipation has bumped that 8 up to a 9 in your mind. If you rate your next visit an 8, the result is that your impression of Disney has been negatively impacted—at least for the present. It's extremely difficult to continue to live up to the excellence you create. This is the dilemma Disney and other Exceptional organizations face 365 days a year. The only way to maintain and deliver the Exceptional on a consistent basis is to be able to derive a culture of excellence and consistency. And as stated before, excellence is not about perfection, but rather the relentless pursuit thereof.

Fort Wilderness

We've seen the same scenario repeated over and over at Disney—that it's difficult to compete with excellence when you're striving for perfection. Consider the following story about the Fort Wilderness Campgrounds at Walt Disney World. A friend of Bruce's was doing some cross-training at Fort Wilderness. At lunch, the trainer took his trainee into the Fort Wilderness cafeteria for cast members. On the wall was a large sign that read, "Guest Satisfaction: 77%." The trainee was quite amazed and asked: "Why is the score so low? I would have expected it to be much higher."

His trainer chuckled and said, "You obviously don't know our system. You see, most companies have a five-level scale of how their customers evaluate service: poor, average, good, very good, and excellent. When *they* report on customer satisfaction, they include good, very good, and excellent in order to arrive at their customer satisfaction. If we did it at the Lodge, our scores would be 97 percent to 99 percent just about every time. If employees feel that we are almost perfect, what incentive is there for them to push themselves to improve? The answer is: very little. At Fort Wilderness, we *only* count those guests who rated us as excellent, so we each have room to grow and improve. Seventy-seven percent of our guests rated us as excellent. That gives us room to grow."

People will rarely rise above the level that you set for them. If they feel they are already Exceptional, then they won't try any harder to improve.

Continuous Improvement

You cannot remain the same; you either grow or you stagnate and begin to die. Treading water is the stage before drowning. Those who grow gradually and progress steadily are the ones who are the most successful. How many times have you heard of a person who was making a living on $25,000, was able to pay bills and live fairly comfortably for years, and one day won millions of dollars in the lottery and in three years went broke and declared bankruptcy? The key to success is almost always steady, continuous improvement in everything you do. The person who won the lottery did not put in the time and effort or receive the education needed to earn that money; therefore, he or she did not have the aptitude to *keep* that money. It's the same for the marketplace and in developing the Exceptional Experience. Slow and steady is what is reproducible and what you can replicate over and over again. Continuous improvement is the personification of excellence.

Everyone can improve. Whether you are in retail, in consulting, in transportation, or are creating Experiences on the Internet, you and your organization must improve, or it will cost you dearly. *Forrester Research found that customer Experience quality could result in a $184 million swing in sales for a certain large Internet-based retailer.* Our customers are paying attention, and they deserve better.

> *Forrester Research found that customer Experience quality could result in a $184 million swing in sales for a certain large Internet-based retailer.*

Be Exceptional!

The United States is truly Exceptional. Never in the history of the world has there been another country that has achieved as much in such a relatively short time. Being Exceptional should always be a source of pride! Celebrate it when you achieve the unthinkable, when you delivered the impossible, or when you were just plain excellent. Strive to be the best you were designed to be, and do not let anyone make you feel guilty for wanting to be Exceptional at what you do and excellent in creating Exceptional Experiences for others.

Quotient Question

Is there a clear commitment to excellence in the organization, and is the pursuit felt in every facet of the "I. C.A.R.E." customer Experience?

Actionables

Excellence is the pursuit of perfection yet the grace to understand that perfection is not possible. In our grasp for perfection, we fall short and still achieve excellence.

(continued)

(*Continued*)

Try this

☞ Identify five specific qualities that relate to service excellence for you and/or your team. Make note of them and then take an in-depth look at the growth over the next quarter, year, and even three years. We have provided more than 50 qualities in this book along with the 5 Principles themselves. You should continue to measure the overall Experience with our Experience Quotient, but pick five qualities that specifically relate to what you define as excellence.

Try this

☞ Create an "excellence meter." The hypothetical measurement tool should gauge the level of excellence in any action on a scale of 1 to 10 and should encompass all of the elements of the five service excellence qualities you have chosen.

Try this

☞ Identify the people in the organization who have the most capacity for growth, and concentrate on them for leadership and in your pursuit of excellence. Create a special group who are clearly establishing themselves as excellent, and begin to develop them for the future.

Exceptionals 5.3:
Ethos

It's not hard to make decisions when you know what your values are.

—Roy E. Disney

Ethos is much more than a brand or a slogan. It is the *why* behind the people, product, and service that the Experience is supporting. Ethos is what you stand for and the secret that the Experience is supporting. It is the character behind your brand—the secret ingredient to your recipe for the Experience.

Disneyland, and ultimately every other Disney park, was designed to be an ongoing, living, permanent show. Walt's dream was to have each guest become part of that live show as he or she enjoyed the various attractions and shows. In order to pull this off, Walt borrowed from the venue with which he was most familiar: movies. He incorporated numerous ideas and even the terminology (as highlighted in an earlier Principle, Connection 2.2, Deliberate) from both the movie and hospitality industries.

The overarching ethos of Disney is to create the happiest place on earth. This mantra and this purpose show up in Disney's strategy, destinations, and even nomenclature. We've touched on this in other chapters, but it's a central facet to Disney's approach. The parks don't have customers; they have "guests." Employees aren't hired for a job in a company; they "audition" for a "role" in the "show." Employees are called "cast members," and uniforms are called "costumes." It may sound odd, but it works—and it's not just a matter of using different words. It truly extends to the meaning and the approach. We've even noticed that companies such as Target and Chick-fil-A have adopted the term *guest* to refer to their customers; and of course, hotels have used the term for years.

There is logic to using the term *guest* versus *customer*. Most companies associate customers with profit or money. And when this association filters down to the frontline employees, it tends to make the interaction impersonal and they often treat customers simply as dollar signs. *According to a Genesys Global Study, by far the most requested improvement from customers (40 percent) was "better human service."* Our customers just want to be treated better. They deserve it, and it begins with an internal ethos.

> *According to a Genesys Global Study, by far the most requested improvement from customers (40 percent) was "better human service."*

When we consider the term *guest*, we tend to see the customer in a new light, similar to how you would view friends who are visiting you in your home. Prior to their visit, wouldn't you clean thoroughly, make a pot of coffee, and perhaps even bake some brownies or cookies? Wouldn't you dress nicely, welcome them in, and offer them a comfortable place to sit? In most cases, the term *guest* could easily be used to replace *customer*, and it would only serve to improve how we perceive and treat them. It's a mindset and an ethos as much as it is simply terminology.

The Why

Possibly the most important question you can ask yourself in any endeavor you pursue is the "why." What is great about knowing the "why" is that it defines the "what," "how," and "who." Your "why" is the foundation for being Exceptional!

When you boil it down, your "why" is merely your purpose, your reason for doing anything. And when your "why" is strong enough, nothing is impossible. That is an important distinction, since your "why's" impact and direct your choices. Mark Twain said it best when he observed, "The two most important days in your life are the day were born and the day you find out why." When your "why" is well-defined, you are then free to do whatever you want within the boundaries of your purpose. In this way, understanding your purpose provides clarity.

Our goal throughout *The Experience* is to provide the "why," the purpose—your reason for excellence. In other words, how do we help take you to the next level? That starts with "why" you desire to be Exceptional in the first place. You've got to find what you love, and what you can commit yourself to, that is bigger than yourself. Find your purpose—your reason for being. That ethos will make all the difference in the world for you and your organization.

Quotient Question

Is there a clear ethos (your *why*) behind the brand and the Experience created by the organization?

Actionables

The most powerful question we can answer is "Why?" Everything we do revolves around the purpose behind why we do it.

Try this

☞ Go back to the basics. In quarterly meetings with your team, department, or organization, brainstorm using the following questions:

1. Why do customers use our product or service?

2. Why have we created this product or service?

(continued)

(*Continued*)

3. Why do we desire to create an Exceptional Experience for our customers?

Try this

☞ For the next month, try calling your customers guests each time you address them or refer to them. The next month, try introducing the concept of onstage as a way to define what professionalism should look like. Try developing your own intellectual property and terminology going forward, and watch what happens to the overall pride and purpose in the Experience offering.

Try this

☞ Identify one thing (individually or as a team) that you do better than anyone else within the organization. Ask yourself what you do that makes you so effective and how you can apply this to other aspects of your service. Even more important, how can you inspire others to raise their game to your level? Remember that people normally are most purposed when they are doing things they are good at.

Exceptionals 5.4:
Accountability

Accountability breeds response-ability.

—Stephen Covey

Accountability and ownership are synonymous. Whether you are a sole proprietor of a business or you belong to an organization of thousands, you cannot have effective strategy or reach measurable goals without someone to champion said goals—or without assigning someone to be responsible for the results. How many times has a manager assigned a project to "everyone"? Most of us know all too well that when *everyone* is responsible, no one is responsible. Being intentionally Exceptional requires that someone specific must always be accountable for success or failure.

Walking or Holding

There is a distinct difference between "walking in accountability" versus holding someone accountable. Holding is one-sided. People want to walk with you to a destination and not necessarily be pushed into performance. This ideal is more than just vernacular. *Walking* infers doing something together, while *holding* implies that someone is doing all of the walking and the other person is only along for the ride. Sometimes accountability is just communicating regularly—not necessarily discussing measurable performance, but just talking. *According to a Therkelsen and Fiebich study, employee satisfaction can be increased by more than 50 percent by simply increasing the communication frequency between employees and their direct supervisors.*

According to a Therkelsen and Fiebich study, employee satisfaction can be increased by more than 50 percent by simply increasing the communication frequency between employees and their direct supervisors.

Bruce likes to tell a specific story that took place in the early days at IBM. One of the top salesmen blew a sale that cost the company $50,000. While that wouldn't be much today, it was a small fortune in the infancy of IBM, and it nearly destroyed the company. The next day, founder and president Tom Watson called the young salesman into his office. The young man said, "I guess you'll want to fire me." Watson barked, "Fire you? Heck no, you're the most valuable salesman in our company. You'll never make that mistake again! Now, I want you to tell everyone else how not to make that mistake." This story is a terrific example of an attitude of optimism and walking in accountability.

Demand or Demonstrate

Walt Disney possessed rare qualities of both creativity and organization. He expected excellence out of each member of his staff and he held them accountable for achieving excellence by first being the portrait of an Ambassador of the Experience who possessed undying optimism, a commitment to hard work, and a penchant for precision. Walt understood that you cannot order excellence from your people from a chair. You create it from within.

Accountability is critical to the success of any organization. The ultimate achievement of any project, product, or process will always be closely linked to the relationship between strategy and a method of accountability for execution.

MBWA

Walt was a big believer in getting to know his guests. He noticed that many of the supervisors and managers at Disneyland would take their lunch breaks and eat at their desks or, worse yet, go off property for lunch. When he discovered this, he quickly changed the policy. Walt expected every supervisor to get out of the office, eat their lunch in the park, mingle with guests, and learn about them—where they were from and what they liked and didn't like about the Disney Experience. What better way to find out what works and what doesn't?

Walt was a perfectionist. He knew that if Disneyland were to be successful, leaders must spend time observing, developing, and coaching the Disney cast members on a daily basis. We believe he was probably the initiator of the management by walking around (MBWA) philosophy that was started in the 1950s. You can't simply sit in a chair and expect excellence. You have to get out there and walk in accountability with the employees of the organization.

Quotient Question

Is there a clear method of accountability in the organization, and how strong is the accountability system for delivering excellence?

Actionables

Accountability is the measurement method tool that helps us achieve the results that we are after.

(continued)

(Continued)

Try this

☞ Create a system where leadership is accountable to the employees—not necessarily something formal but a method of displaying goal achievement or performance metrics where the employees of the organization have a clear view into whether the leaders are executing at a high level.

Try this

☞ Identify one person who understands your specific role in the organization, and meet with him or her regularly for the accountability of goal setting, goal achievement, service excellence, and personal growth. Leadership should encourage and in some cases facilitate this happening within an organization.

Try this

☞ Make it a priority and even go as far to mandate that every leader spends time in and among the employee and client base on a weekly basis. This is the best way to observe, to walk in accountability, and to make sure that leadership is aware of what level of Experience is being provided for the customers and employees of the organization.

Exceptionals 5.5:
Teaming

Individual commitment to a group effort, that's what makes a team work, a company work, a society work, a civilization work.

—Vince Lombardi

We believe that each of us was specifically designed to work with others to fulfill a great purpose. Some may think we are over-romanticizing our respective roles as workers in the marketplace and Ambassadors of the Experience, but we do not think so. All through our lives, we have been inspired by the notion that we can be anything we want to be. While we do not want to rain on anyone's parade with this notion, we want to introduce an even more exciting thought. Instead of being anything you want to be, how about falling in love with who you were *designed* to be?

Each of us was born with a certain set of qualities in our DNA that are unique to you and no one else. Finding these unique attributes for yourself and for your fellow employees is one of our Exceptionals that we call teaming. It takes a team to put together an Exceptional Experience. In the concert of tactics that it takes to pull off the Exceptional, you can never accomplish a feat of excellence with a symphony of one.

Hire Right

Disney does this first and probably foremost by hiring the right people. Bruce had the opportunity to work in Disney World's Casting Building when it first opened. In the year he was there, he hired over 500 cast members. The key attributes he would always look for in a potential employee were strong goal orientation, the right attitude, and a desire to serve others. Did they possess the Disney brand of outlook that was personable, outgoing, friendly, and enthusiastic? Did they seem to have the desire to work hard and give their best? Did they have specific goals in life that they wanted to achieve? It they didn't possess all of those qualities, he often felt they wouldn't be a good fit within Disney World.

Bruce takes the same approach that many other wise managers do; that is, we should hire for attitude first and for knowledge and skills second. A good trainer can teach you the skills and provide the necessary knowledge to do the job well—but no one can alter someone else's personality. There is an old National Basketball Association (NBA) scout maxim that states: "You can't coach height." Well, it's our opinion that you hire the right attitude and desire, and you coach the intangibles of skill, knowledge, and process. If someone is an angry, rude, abrasive, condescending, or negative person *before* being hired, there is a strong probability that he or she will be that type of person after coming aboard the team.

How many times have we found a well-meaning manager who hired someone based on skills only to find that the employee was a terrible fit and totally destroyed the chemistry of the team? We can't place enough emphasis on the need for coworkers with a great attitude who are able to get along well with each of their teammates.

Not everyone who applies for a job at your company will be a good fit for the company or for the work that is required. It is much better to learn that fact at the start than well down the road. *According to a Wood Associates study, burnout is the number one cause of employee turnover, not*

> *According to a Wood Associates study, burnout is the number one cause of employee turnover, not to mention that employee turnover costs an organization 5.8 percent of its annual budget.*

to mention that employee turnover costs an organization 5.8 percent of its annual budget. Hiring right to make sure that a team is in place that creates synergy and efficiencies is profitable not only to the Experience but also to the wallet of the organization.

When Walt Disney World opened in 1971, it was hiring only one out of every 12 applicants who "auditioned" for a job there, so the park had the freedom to be extremely selective about who was hired. By 1989, that ratio had changed dramatically to one out of every 2.1 applicants. This clearly shows that the caliber of new hires wasn't nearly as high in 1989 as it had been in 1971. I believe it is now around one out of every 4.5, which is about where it should be. Some of those new hires went on to become leaders and supervisors and managers. The key for Disney and for your company is to get the right people and the best people in the right positions to begin with.

Hire Your Profile Client

If you could design an employee who would be capable of creating the Exceptional Experience for your customers, who would it be? There is an easy answer: it would be the customers themselves. They know what they want; they know how to communicate with themselves and those like them; and they will empathize directly with those who have the same wants, desires, and needs.

In doing research for this book, I was able to spend some time with the former CEO at Tractor Supply, Joe Scarlett. As we toured one of the facilities one day, Joe began to introduce me to a few of the employees and managers. It was amazing: almost every one of them grew up on a farm or had significant exposure to a rural lifestyle while growing up. This is a perfect example of the type of teaming that should take place within your organization. If you hire those people who think, live, and purchase the same way that your clients do, the Experience cannot help but to be enhanced.

Casting

People are hired at Disney for a specific role. Disney does not have "jobs," but every cast member is "auditioned" and selected to fit a "role" or a "part" in the Disney show. Even the Casting Center prepares prospective new hires for the role they will be playing as a Disney cast member. In Lake Buena Vista, the Casting Center—or as cast members refer to it, "The Argyle Building"—is pure fantasy in itself. It was designed by world-famous architect Robert Stern to impress new hires and to provide a glimpse of what a magical place Disney would be for them to work. The walls leading up a long ramp to the second floor display whimsical murals of various Disney characters with statues sitting atop columns.

Of course, not all companies are able to hire world-class architects to build their buildings. But any business is capable of communicating its ethos and values to the inside and outside world through its actions and words.

Green Side Up

We recently had the opportunity to sit down with one of Bruce's dear friends and mentors, Spencer Craig. Dr. Craig is best known for his work in merchandising for the Walt Disney Company as well as being a former manager of Disney University. He told us a story about the evening before the grand opening of the Contemporary Hotel at Disney World in 1971. The entire management team had to lay sod to make sure that the hotel was ready in time. The ordeal lasted into the next morning, when fatigue began to set in. Suffice to say that the individuals laying the sod were having a very hard time concentrating on the quality of their sodding prowess.

Dick Nunis (future president at Disney and Spencer's boss at the time) bought the team T-shirts after the ordeal that read "Green

Side Up!" This slogan commemorated the team's effort but also their exhaustion in the endeavor. This is a tremendous example of casting the right people: team members who would not allow the Experience for their future guests to be affected by a lack of sod being in place; team members who were willing to forget their titles and agendas to simply get the job done. This is a commitment to excellence and the Experience that can be trained and encouraged but is usually hired and then cultivated.

The emphasis on the right people to build the right team is of utmost importance at Disney, as it should be in your organization. We must be able to connect as a team and with our frontline employees before we ever can be ready to connect with our customers. Remember, you have more than one shot at excellence—but you have only one opportunity to help employees find their destiny and to build relationships within a team that are capable of unlocking an incredible Experience.

Quotient Question

Do you feel that you have the right people in the right places at the right times in order to execute the Experience with precision?

Actionables

Our level of success depends on the selection of teammates and then the ability of the team to work together and support each other.

Try this

☞ Make a profile of your prototypical client and then make it a priority to hire similar people. Look for those people who

(*continued*)

(Continued)

match the Experience you have built. Hire those who have the same values, needs, and likes as the customers, and watch the Experience be enhanced to a level you never thought possible.

Try this

☞ Once a quarter, gather the team and create an exercise to promote each of their strengths. Each person has a fit. Everyone was designed for greatness in some way. Celebrate these strengths and the fit of the team. Introduce ways to teach the team, department, or organization to rely on the various attributes of the team to execute.

Try this

☞ Once a quarter, get the various members of the organization or team together to have fun. Work can be fun, but it is also imperative to get everyone outside the lines of the organization to have a good time and engage in team-building activities.

Exceptionals 5.6:
Investment

Transformation in the world happens when people are healed and start investing in other people.

—Michael W. Smith

One of the most important things you can do for yourself, or for anyone else, is to invest in them. Life is about growing and improving—and if you are not helping others grow, there is a void that will affect the organization as a whole. The term *atrophy* is very appropriate here: what you don't use, you lose. If, for instance, you were to tie your arm to your body for six months and never to use it, the muscles in your arm would atrophy, rendering it useless, possibly for the rest of your life.

The cerebral component is also at stake here. There are many areas and forms of cerebral stimulus that can and should take place to help the team grow. It is the responsibility of leadership to invest in the components to avoid atrophy of the mind and spirit. Just like your muscles, your brain must be challenged, stretched, and exercised on a regular basis.

Consistent Investment

Investment speaks to the amount of effort, development, love, and encouragement you put into employees and deliverers of the Experience. Your people will treat your customers the same way they are treated, so the investment in the employee must equal the investment into the consumer. Your primary purpose on earth is to improve yourself and to improve others. You achieve this by investing time, vision, and knowledge on a frequent basis.

In a recent study conducted by the ROI Institute, it was found that only 8 percent of the CEOs measured their investment in leadership development programs and how they helped improve business performance and employee retention. If you are dedicated and intentional about investing in your people and coworkers, and you do it on a consistent basis, you will most definitely see a return on your investment. You must continue to do the fundamental things—the right things—day after day, and be intentional about measuring the results.

> *In a recent study conducted by the ROI Institute, it was found that only 8 percent of the CEOs measured their investment in leadership development programs and how they helped improve business performance and employee retention.*

No Ivory Towers

I have been blessed to spend a good amount of time with the former CEO of Tractor Supply, Joe Scarlett. Not only is the company one of the masters of the external Experience, but it also has mastered the art of rising up internal Ambassadors of the organization and investing in the internal Experience as well. During Joe's tenure at Tractor Supply, the company went from $330 million in sales in 1994 to more than $2.4 billion in total revenue in 2006. Asked how this was possible, Joe gave the credit to his people, to his customers, and to the creation of an Exceptional Experience for the "hobby farmer."

Joe also began to explain to me the difference in the company's mentality of how it appreciates, supports, and invests in its leaders and employees, down to the terminology for the home office in Brentwood, Tennessee. The people at Tractor Supply do not call it a "home office" at all; they call it the "store support center." No ivory towers there. Doesn't that sound like a company you would like to work with?

Building Experts

Inspirational and motivational thinker Earl Nightingale once stated that if you dedicate one hour per day, seven days per week, 365 days per year to the study of a topic, any topic, you will be as knowledgeable about that subject in five years as any expert in that field. Again, it's the idea that consistency and intentionality make you a success. That is how people become experts and how employees become Ambassadors. If you dedicate yourself and your organization to the development of experts and Ambassadors, the investment will certainly yield a greater internal and external Experience and show up in the growth of the organization.

There is a concept that we like to employ with regard to investing in others that we call being "altruistically selfish." This involves training your brain to invest in yourself and your organization by making it your culture and your mantra to pour everything back into the people who serve the organization and its customers. Life isn't about what you get, but rather what you give that makes you successful. Those who are often the happiest, most fulfilled, and the most productive are those who invest in others and help them succeed. The "altruistically selfish" ideal is undefeated. Try it!

Quotient Question

How well do employees feel that they are being developed, encouraged, and invested in both personally as well as professionally?

Actionables

The ability to invest in ourselves and in others provides a return that is greater than any monetary investment.

Try this

☞ Have a book of the month or book of the quarter club. Each member of the team or the organization (on behalf of the team) purchases an inspirational or instructional book that will add value to the overall execution level of the organization and the personal growth of the employees.

Try this

☞ Create a monthly or quarterly recognition program. Find ways to create competition, contests, bonuses, and recognition on a regular basis. Tie the awards with the needed results and the strategy of the organization. It's a win-win for everyone!

Try this

☞ Survey the employee base and ask people specifically what they think of themselves as or what area want to become an expert in. Then make the effort to prepare them, coach them, and develop them within this arena. The more experts you have, the greater the opportunity to have an organization that takes pride in the Experience it offers to customers and clients.

Exceptionals 5.7:
Training

Excellence is an art won by training and habituation.

—Aristotle

Disney keeps its level of excellence intact through a commitment of investing in its people and through ongoing training. When Bruce created his position as a service excellence coordinator at Disney, he developed specific "cast rehearsal classes" (CRCs). In order to keep the Disney cast up to speed and in top shape, class leaders would periodically rehearse cast members' roles with them in order to fine-tune the show and to define their expectations of excellence. The idea was to instill pride into each member of the Disney cast, as it always would come out in their performance onstage. CRCs were usually done with no more than five cast members at a time and often one-on-one for more personalized training and development.

The Ambassadors of the Experience must be prepared. Without preparation, you cannot hold them accountable for executing the Experience. Training is one of the most intentional tools we have at our disposal. It enables us to establish expectations and also to create a mold and a model of what leaders want, need, and expect from every employee. Without it, Disney and countless other Exceptional brands would not and could not be as consistent or effective as they are.

Know Your Stuff

An essential part of executing the Experience is to have employees who know everything they can know about the products and services that make up the presentation and the deliverable. Few things are more frustrating to a customer than to ask an employee about products or services and receive the reply, "I don't know." It is acceptable to say, "I am not sure, but I will find out"; however, if the employees are not experts in their field of work, why are they there interfacing with your customers in the first place?

One of the many things Bruce appreciated about Disney is that every single employee was indoctrinated with the brand's history and culture. They were taught how Walt got his start in 1923 and what a great company they were now a part of. Bruce used to tell new cast members, "Your first day of work will be your most exciting because you finally will get to be part of this great company." This internal Experience set the stage for the cast members at Disney to have a certain hunger for knowledge and to become true Ambassadors of the brand they represented. The better equipped and prepared the employees are, the better chance you will have at delivering the Exceptional Experience.

Connect the Dots

Every employee in your company needs to know how his or her job is directly linked to customer satisfaction. They need to be able to connect the dots and define how their efforts either directly interface with or support those individuals who have direct contact with the customer.

We like to talk about customizing the Experience, but what our customers want most is competency and knowledge. *According to a Genesys Global Study,*

> *According to a Genesys Global Study, 78 percent of consumers prefer competent service reps over personalization of service.*

78 percent of consumers prefer competent service reps over personalization of service. Competency comes from preparation and training, and that is what a firm foundational Experience is erected from.

Training

Disney places a great deal of time and effort into training. After Traditions, new employees are released into the area they will be working in. A trainer then spends a day with them to introduce them to coworkers and show them everything about their new area. They discuss duties and processes. Training often lasts between one week and two weeks before new employees are tested to determine whether they know their responsibilities and can be put on the floor.

These are some of the most critical days for a new cast member. Disney clearly puts a lot emphasis on portraying a role or position within the company. In those roles, there were and are specific expectations that are required of every cast member: be friendly, smile, make eye contact, greet or welcome guests, be courteous, offer assistance, and thank every guest when they leave. Some of those skills are not natural for many new cast members who join the Disney team.

That is where intense Disney training enters the picture. Not only must new cast members learn everything about their new job; they must also learn and consistently demonstrate "the Disney way" about being genuine and friendly with every guest. Every new cast member has been hired to fit within the Disney model of service and excellence. But, without proper training and preparation, it would be impossible for a new cast member to effectively fit into the role of being a Disney cast member.

Ongoing Training

Most people could call this "ongoing training," but Bruce calls it "rehearsing the show." No matter how long you do a job, it can become routine, dull, and boring to any employee, which then translates to a "poor show." After a cast member has received initial training and has been on the job for six months or a year, it can be very beneficial to offer additional, enhanced training in order to fine-tune the show. Part of the internal Experience is making the employees feel that they are important. *According to an InteliSpend survey, 39 percent of employees feel underappreciated at work, with 77 percent reporting that they would work harder if they felt better recognized.* We have to invest, recognize, and empower our people. There is perhaps no better way to achieve a positive internal Experience than to be a conduit to the advancement of our people through training.

According to an Inteli-Spend survey, 39 percent of employees feel under-appreciated at work, with 77 percent reporting that they would work harder if they felt better recognized.

The military calls these "exercises" and "war games"; at Disney, it is called "rehearsing." More than training, this involves preparing the staff to be ready and prepared for any situation that may arise. In these cases, role-playing offers an excellent opportunity to train cast members about what to do in the event of storms, power outages, accidents, evacuations, and a multitude of other unforeseen circumstances that may impact their work. Without ongoing and refresher training, many of the cast members would not be ready for a major event—and the same likely goes for your employees.

Be Teachable

Whether we are frontline employees or in management, we all have to learn from others. No one is that good that they can do it all on their own. Other people are there to help us and serve as examples of what works and what doesn't. We all need guides and mentors along the way who act as coaches to create guidelines and boundaries that provide focus and direction. Those who are truly great at delivering the Experience and who have attained a high degree of wisdom are those who have become sponges to absorb truths and understanding along the way. Know-it-alls display an arrogance that demonstrates their unteachable nature. Only those who are teachable are the ones who have the capacity for growth.

Quotient Question

Is the organization providing the proper training for personal development and for performing the responsibilities necessary to create a positive customer Experience?

Actionables

Training is the blueprint behind the Experience that the organization will deliver. Training is the road map to the level of excellence that you will ultimately deliver to the customer.

Try this

☞ Review the current training programs and identify one of the key components that could become more prominent. Ask yourself, "What is one thing that leadership can do to better train in this important area?" Focus on the ultimate goal of yielding a greater Experience for the employees and the clients.

Try this

☞ Encourage and underwrite the use of outside education as a way to better empower employees. Whether it be higher education, continuing education, or credentialing, the Experience for the employee is enhanced with this type of encouragement and commitment from the organization.

(*continued*)

(Continued)

Try this

☞ Create special recognition for your levels of continuing education and training. Disney has Disney University. What do you have? Draw awareness to the necessity to desire growth and knowledge. Encourage it through quotes, exercises, retreats, and various other awareness tactics.

Exceptionals 5.8:
Development

The growth and development of people [are] the highest calling of leadership.

—Harvey Firestone

The source of all growth is dissatisfaction and desire. As long as you are satisfied with the status quo, you will never see reason to change. You cannot become what you were destined to be until you are first unhappy with where you are. Therefore, personal and people development can be found only on the other side of the desire to grow.

The foundation to personal development is discipline. Most of us do not grow in quantum leaps, but rather in incremental amounts—what we call "baby steps." In order to sustain personal growth, we typically get there via gradual steps that lay a firm foundation, and then we build upon those small steps. Just as we do not ask organizations to move up more than one level of the Experience hierarchy at a time, we also should not expect individuals to develop those excellence muscles overnight. These baby steps can be taken by developing and following specific goals, displaying the appropriate level of commitment, and then having the discipline to execute day in and day out.

Next, there must be passion to change. It's extremely difficult to imagine Henry Ford, Thomas Edison, Walt Disney, John D. Rockefeller, or J. P. Morgan accomplishing all they did without having a passion for the future. It was what motivated all of them to the relentless development of their craft. Ultimate change comes when we are all in and determined to accept nothing less than excellence—personally as well as professionally.

The ability to be Exceptional is locked inside of everyone. You and your people's main priority is to find that hidden power and expose it. You are already ahead of the game if you recognize that it exists; however, you'll be able to let it loose only by making a deliberate decision to develop the talent, skills, and Exceptionals within the organization.

Goals

In 1953, a group of researchers interviewed the graduating class of the Harvard School of Business. They found that only 3 percent had long-range, written, specific goals; 10 percent had "generic goals"; and the remaining 87 percent had no goals, other than to graduate from the business school. The researchers stayed in contact with the graduates, and in 1978, 25 years later, they interviewed them again—and the results were nothing short of phenomenal. The 3 percent who had had long-range, written, specific goals had a net worth greater than the other 97 percent combined. That is an incredible statistic, since many of the 97 percent were successful in their own right.

In 1953, a group of researchers interviewed the graduating class of the Harvard School of Business. They found that only 3 percent had long-range, written, specific goals; 10 percent had "generic goals"; and the remaining 87 percent had no goals, other than to graduate from the business school.

Finding your fit means discovering what you were designed to do and pouring yourself into it with every ounce of energy in your being. Having well-defined, written goals will help you achieve that.

Discipleship as the Key

The best way to bring people along in the cultural and tactical aspects of your organization is to have someone who has mastered the internal arts walk with them through their respective roles. *According to Aberdeen, 89 percent of employers assume that their employees leave for more money elsewhere, but only 12 percent of employees actually earn more from their next company.* Employees are not usually leaving a company; they are often leaving their boss due to a lack of communication or a lack of development. The idea is to train individuals by first teaching them, then by showing them specifically how it is done, and then finally by observing them in action. This method of teach/show/observe is not new. It's something that Disney and other great organizations have used for decades.

Discipleship is an appropriate word to use when we are describing the development of people. If you have a specific level of excellence and an ethos built upon strong cultural concepts, discipleship is the best way to duplicate your greatest people. Truly, it is the only way to create internal Ambassadors. The word *disciple* itself means to be a pupil of or an adherent to the doctrines or ideas of another. We would not necessarily go as far as to say that you are creating disciples of the Experience; but in converting employees to Ambassadors, the concept of discipleship is a proven method that will be invaluable in developing the future talent in your organization.

Quotient Question

Is there a system of apprenticeship and goal execution that is a part of your training program?

Actionables

Employee and leadership development is the hallmark of a great organization.

Try this

☞ Identify the one thing you or the team does not particularly like. Concentrate on items that have a direct effect on the customer Experience. For the next 30 days, work on your levels of execution, enthusiasm, and commitment to better this one area of disdain. If you can gain capacity for the items you dislike, you can truly develop the Exceptional.

Try this

☞ Select a project or goal that is important to you. Apply the S.M.A.R.T. Goal principle:

S. ~ Specific: It should be well defined.

M. ~ Measurable: Devise a way to benchmark your progress.

A. ~ Achievable: Make it feasible.

R. ~ Relevant: Is it important to you and will it make a difference?

T. ~ Time framed: Does it have a beginning date and an end date?

Try this

☞ Promote discipleship (duplication of talent) in pairs within the organization. Leaders should find employees in the

(continued)

(Continued)

organization who could use their guidance and support. Before asking if they need help, offer ideas or suggestions that would help them in their work or attitude. If they are receptive and implement your ideas and you feel a connection, ask if they would be interested in you giving them personal direction. Mentoring is about paying it forward and investing in others as others have invested in you.

Exceptionals 5.9:
Extraordinary

People do not decide to become extraordinary. They decide to accomplish extraordinary things.

—Edmund Hillary

People deserve a better Experience. When we believe this, the Exceptional Experience becomes possible. To strive to be extraordinary is a unique feat in itself. In our research for and through our process of writing this book, we have identified a few extra items that certain organizations (like Disney) possess and strive for that set them apart. They believe that people deserve better, and these attributes provide the path to the extraordinary.

Dream

Every great inventor and entrepreneur was at first laughed at, mocked, belittled, and labeled a failure. Consider what people like Walt Disney, Henry Ford, Thomas Edison, Benjamin Franklin, Albert Einstein, Alexander Graham Bell, and hundreds of others went through. All of them heard multiple times that their dreams were impractical and a waste of time. Yet, had they not had the fortitude, determination, perseverance, and vision, we would not have some of the greatest ideas and inventions the world has ever known.

> *It has been said that at age 5, you will have the most creativity you will ever have, but by age 21, you will have lost 95 percent of that creativity.*

The ability to dream and add momentum to your dream is an invaluable tool. *It has been said that at age 5, you will have the most creativity you will ever have, but by age 21, you will have lost 95 percent of that creativity.* What happens between the age of 5 and the age of 21? Structured education. Our educational system is constantly placing boundaries around what is right and wrong, and everything must fit within the educators' expectations. At first Einstein and Edison were labeled failures because they didn't fit within the normal range of thinking.

In 1843, the U.S. Patent Office was rumored to not allow any additional patents because it felt that nothing else needed to be patented—everything that needed to be invented had *already* been invented. This line of thinking was later reversed as Chairman Charles H. Duell stated, "Our future progress and prosperity depend upon our ability to equal, if not surpass, other nations in the enlargement and advance of science, industry, and commerce. To invention we must turn as one of the most powerful aids to the accomplishment of such a result." You see, dreaming is the catalyst for invention.

The part of our brain known as the prefrontal cortex controls the executive functions—decision making, futuristic thought, vision casting, working toward a defined goal, and the orchestration of actions in accordance with internal goals. In other words, it is the part of our brain that does the heavy lifting when it comes to producing a purpose, pursuing goals, and turning a dream for the future into a present reality.

Like most muscles in the human body, if you do not exercise that specific part of the anatomy, it will atrophy. In this case, if you don't exercise your "vision muscles," you will lose the ability to dream big, as well as the ability to push those dreams into reality.

Innovate

Innovation often begins with getting out of your rut. You know what is wrong with your department, your company, and your industry; it's now your job to do something about it. Start writing blogs, articles, or manuals that demonstrate how to take service, products, and customers into the twenty-first century. Do as every great inventor and entrepreneur has done: find a need and fill it. Or even better, *create* a need and completely blow up the market. Constantly ask yourself: how can this be improved?

Bruce has a good friend named Michael LeBoeuf who served as his inspiration to write his first book, *One Minute Service* (DC Press, 2009). Michael used to be the professor of management at New Orleans University. He suggests two critical questions that everyone should ask of themselves every day: "How are we doing?" and "How can we get better?" Can you imagine how your world would improve if you were able to ask those two questions, in some form or another, of every customer, of every coworker, and of your boss? The sky would be the limit for you, your growth, and your potential.

The saying "nothing ventured, nothing gained" is absolutely true. You will never reach second base if you always keep one foot planted on first. Remember, the greatest successes in life are often derived from a foundation set by the greatest failures. Risk is a major part of success. Remember, a ship moored in the harbor is safe, but it will never achieve the purpose it was designed for. You can't imagine a 747 jet driving down the interstate. You have been endowed with certain talents, and it is your purpose in life to discover your gifts and become fulfilled in utilizing them. Innovate on!

The Extra Mile

You may not be aware of the origin of the term *extra mile*. Two thousand years ago, Rome had conquered the known world. One of those conquered territories was Judea, which is known today as Israel.

The Romans had a law stating that any Roman soldier could order any Jewish boy to carry the soldier's backpack for one mile. The backpacks of a Roman soldier often weighed 60 or 70 pounds and the Jewish boys often weighed somewhere around the same. If a Jewish boy refused, it could be immediate grounds for death.

The Rabbis of the land got together and sent out an edict to all Jewish boys. It was the law that the boy must carry the backpack for one mile, but at the end of that mile, he should politely ask, "Could I carry this an extra mile for you?" The Roman soldier was in control during the first mile, because he had the power and the authority. But who was in control the second mile? The Jewish boy—because he chose, of his own free will, to go that extra mile. It is often the choice that we make to go the extra mile, to do the little things that often make the greatest difference, that places us in control of our own destiny!

Most people are not willing to go the extra mile. You won't find much competition against you when you choose to do other things that people are not willing to make the sacrifice to do. You do not need to be a star or a millionaire or the president of a company to go the extra mile; unassuming, hardworking individuals who refuse to settle for Average do it every single day.

The Extra Mile Principle can apply to everything you do—when you pick up after someone who dropped litter, when you help a coworker who is overwhelmed with the task ahead, when you offer to mow an elderly neighbor's yard, and a myriad of other opportunities that we are faced with every day.

Many years ago, an elderly woman was browsing in a department store in Pittsburgh. She was casually strolling through the aisles and would occasionally look at a display case and then move on. None of the employees bothered to ask if she needed help; after all, she seemed to be just looking. After 90 minutes, a young man approached her and asked if he could assist her. She said, "No, but thank you. I'm just waiting for the bus." He then got a chair and asked if she wouldn't like to sit while she waited. When the bus arrived, he took her arm and escorted her to the bus stop. Before she departed, she asked him for a business card.

Two months later, the store manager received a nice letter from the elderly woman requesting this young man to come to her house for an order. The manager informed her that the young man no longer worked at the store, but he would be happy to send another salesperson. The elderly woman stated emphatically, "No, he is the only person I want. Please find him!"

The manager located the former employee and sent him to the woman's home. When he arrived she said, "I would like for you to travel to Scotland and order furniture for my home." Upon his journey to Scotland, he arrived at the Skibo Castle and ordered several hundred thousand dollars of furniture, worth millions in today's dollars. By the way, the elderly woman happened to be the mother of Andrew Carnegie, the wealthiest man in the United States.

The Path

People certainly have a tendency to overcomplicate things at times. This book has put forth a great deal of advice, suggestions, and examples—so much so that one may feel that developing the ultimate Experience is out of reach or so meticulous that one would not even want to begin to climb the mountain. This is not the case. You certainly don't need to try to master all 5 of our I. C.A.R.E. Principles at once; that would be impossible. Just pick a few items and Principles to tackle, and watch the Experience you are delivering and your organization as a whole transform into what you have dared to envision.

The path to the extraordinary is found through a belief that achieving it is possible and that people deserve better than the status quo. The path is then forged specifically with a dream, courage, and the will to innovate, and then a commitment to do what most people and companies simply will not: to go the extra mile!

Quotient Question

Are the employees empowered to create the Experience, and do deliverers of the Experience have the ability to make decisions, innovate, and change?

Actionables

Extraordinary people always go above and beyond to do the things that average people aren't willing to do. Empower your people to perform the Exceptional!

Try this

☞ Hold quarterly brainstorming sessions as to how the Experience can transcend the current one and that of your competition. Get the team and the entire organization involved, as it builds a sense of ownership, camaraderie, and enthusiasm within the group. Analyze what is missing in the service your company provides. Find out what is missing from making the Experience exceptional. This is the time to dream; do not miss the opportunity to take advantage of the creativity and the Exceptional ideas within your organization.

Try this

☞ Look for fresh, innovative ways to make your internal and external Experience Exceptional. Derive a list of new, innovative ideas that are coming from your brainstorming sessions, and try to implement something new each quarter.

Try this

☞ Create an "Extra Mile Award." We have described in other Actionables the process of discussing service highlights within the team. Employees love recognition, and strong leaders love to recognize Exceptional work.

Exceptionals 5.10:
Enjoyment

Enjoyment is an incredible energizer to the human spirit.

—John C. Maxwell

Most employees will tell you that the primary reason they stay with a particular company is *not* the pay, the work, or even the company itself. Rather, it is their boss and colleagues. Many of us spend more time with our associates and our boss than we do with our family. It is imperative that you get along with those you work with in order to enjoy your job and be happy at work. Therefore, we have identified three elements at Disney that add to the level of enjoyment in the workplace: trust, encouragement, and fulfillment.

Trust

When employees develop a sense of trust in their workplace, they feel the freedom to let down their guard and often become more productive and creative. The culture of any organization is the core of what that company is. When leaders feel that they can trust you and when you feel you can trust leadership, innovation happens—and that is a difficult bond to break.

Encouragement

There are many forms of encouragement. Verbal encouragement is always welcomed, as it provides validation to the person receiving it.

Sometimes encouragement comes from someone's presence alone—knowing that a teammate is there if needed or simply takes an interest in your project.

Encouragement is a cultural concept. It drives an organization, it builds momentum within the relational construct of a company, and it is the most valuable currency in an organization.

Another form of encouragement is recognition, or the giving of credit. People like to be acknowledged and thanked for the work they've done and the effort they've put forth. There are few things that can threaten an organization's internal temperature or Experience as much as neglecting to give people credit or taking credit when the praise should be shared. The best leaders—in management or not—are the ones who give all the credit to the team when things go well and absorb all of the blame when things go poorly.

Fulfillment

The secret of enjoyment is fulfillment. Do you and your people believe that you are making the world a better place, and that your customers and clients appreciate what you do? Anything you do for a living is worth doing with enjoyment. *According to our research, 78 percent of employees say it is more important to enjoy work and be happy on the job than it is to make a lot of money.*

According to our research, 78 percent of employees say it is more important to enjoy work and be happy on the job than it is to make a lot of money.

The key ingredient here is doing what you love, because you will most certainly be better at that than at something that you have no passion for. Getting people into the right roles, and then helping them set achievable goals where they are praised for their execution, is the recipe for fulfillment in the marketplace.

If your or your organization's value proposition deals with the delivery of a customer Experience, it is impossible to execute on an above-average deliverable without the leadership and employees enjoying what they are doing. Even the greatest poker players in the world cannot hide dissatisfaction. The way that the employees, your Ambassadors of the Experience, are treated and their level of enjoyment will show up in the relational elements of service and in the client Experience.

Remember: what happens backstage will eventually end up onstage. The Experience and the environment created for the employees of the company will directly correlate with the Experience that is delivered for the customer. It takes more effort and frequently more capital to create an environment of trust, fulfillment, and encouragement than it does to create their antithetical partners of distrust, emptiness, and discouragement. However, have you ever counted the cost of not creating a positive environment? Do you truly desire to create an Exceptional Experience for your customers? If so, start with those who matter most: your people, your internal Ambassadors, and your coworkers. Invest in them, listen to them, prepare them, and most certainly empower them, and you can do what many believe to be impossible: you *will* create the Exceptional.

Quotient Question

Is there a positive atmosphere within the organization, and do employees feel the freedom to have fun and enjoy their work?

Actionables

We tend to make life and work far too stressful. Look for, discover, and create the enjoyment and fun within your work.

Try this

☞ Every day, look for ways to affirm and build up your fellow employees. Set a goal (each day) to give one compliment to

(*continued*)

(Continued)

each fellow employee you come in contact with. Imagine what work would be like if everyone did this.

Try this

☞ Be creative; come up with three phrases that you can use with customers that will enable you to play and lighten the atmosphere so that you can both have fun in your work. Share these as a team and post them. This may sound elementary, but if it's out of sight, it often cannot be ingrained in the mind.

Try this

☞ Make sure that files exist documenting employees' strengths, motivations, and goals. Leadership and employees need to understand the various elements that motivate and add to the fulfillment of fellow employees. The team, the individuals, and the organization will benefit greatly when specific fulfillment items are shared with the group. This builds relational momentum and enjoyment within the workplace.

Chapter Nine
Finale: The One Level Challenge

What about You or Your Company Says, "I. C.A.R.E."?

Accept the challenges so that you may feel the exhilaration of victory.

—George S. Patton

The purpose of this book—truly, this tool—is to help our readers develop relational Experiences. The consumer or client must develop a cerebral Connection with the product, company, or service, as well as the people involved. Interestingly, the word *relationship* itself is derived from the Middle English word *relacion*, meaning a restoration, a mode of relation, and a significant association among people.

The Experience you are committed to causing—and the actual Experience you instigate—is the catalyst to building a lasting relationship with consumers. The objective is to attract customers *to* an Experience, engage in a relationship *through* an Experience, and then convert them to lifelong Ambassadors *of* the Experience. Without a relational connection, there can be no loyalty generated, and therefore it would be theoretically impossible to convert customers to Ambassadors.

It should be clear by this point that Ambassadors are needed for growth and to expand an organization's market and brand awareness. But why is it an absolute necessity for survival to create the best possible Experience for clients and customers? There are three reasons:

1. **People deserve better.** If you do not believe this, then you simply cannot deliver the excellence needed for the Exceptional. It all starts with the Experience that you are committed to providing others.

At some point in time, many American organizations began to shift toward a new mindset. They began to adopt a mentality of delivering "less than you expect and more than you deserve." While you'd never find this slogan hanging over the doorway in a break room, you do find it in the attitude and approach of countless employees. The quality of customer service and relationally based Experiences has been declining for years.

We believe it is time for a value and Experiential renaissance. We have provided an examination of Disney and its mastery of the Experience. We have looked into some of the beliefs and tactics of a few of the other great organizations within the United States and how they are delivering the Exceptional. And one of the things that these great organizations have in common is their relentless resolve to delivering an Exceptional Experience, and a belief that their clients and customers simply deserve the best in service and in life. It's a mindset set according to which they are constantly operating.

2. **Competition.** There are far too many choices and there is far too much information available to potential consumers for anyone to deliver something less than Great. The customer has abundant choices, and providing Average or Toxic service could be the death knell for your organization.

When Walt Disney World opened in 1971, there was little competition for the park. In 1975, Sea World opened in Orlando, and Universal Studios opened in 1989. Then came Wet 'n Wild, Ripley's Believe It or Not, Medieval Times, and multiple other competitors to the Disney parks. Individually, none of them could compete with Disney World, but each began to chip away from Disney's base of guests. Even Disney had to concentrate on making its Experience one of escalating demand to fend off its competitors.

Jeff Gregoire said it best when he commented, "The customer experience is the next competitive battleground." There is simply too much information and too many strong alternatives to not pay close attention to your service and relational Connection models. Nothing provides a greater Impression or Connection than that of a positive Experience. The customer has a choice, but so do you. You can choose to be intentional about gaining or protecting market share through your efforts to deliver the Exceptional.

3. **Ambassadors.** Our customers, clients, and consumers desire an Experience; they are aware of the Experience they come into contact with (positive or negative), and they will most certainly share their Experience with others.

As we have discussed throughout the book, the power of the crowd is a difference maker in and for any organization. An Exceptional or Great Experience will yield Ambassadors who are dedicated to sharing their positive Experience with the world. An Average or Toxic Experience will yield the opposite result: you will not only lose out on the opportunity to create viral growth and favorable free press, but you will also create detractors to the brand.

Remember: for every complaint that you receive, there are roughly 26 other dissatisfied customers who remained silent—at least silent to you and your organization. You'd better believe that they are telling someone. You see, American consumers tell between five and nine people about a positive Experience but, as stated in the story of Bruce's Experience with Motel "X," they will tell as many as 16 people about their negative Experience. The key here is to understand that you actually will be creating either Ambassadors or anti-Ambassadors. Whether the word of mouth will be positive or negative is up to you.

The Next Level

The Experience is dedicated to helping each organization achieve the next level of the Experience it can create for its employees and customers alike. So how do we get to the next level? You'll recall our earlier discussion about the five things your company must focus on to dramatically alter your business and image. These I. C.A.R.E. Principles—and their 50 supporting sub-Principles—are the very elements and opportunities that can help you enhance the Experience and become the person and organization you have envisioned.

Every organization faces obstacles, pressures on market share, and narrowing margins due to the commoditization of their business. The greatest way to protect yourself and your organization from losing market share and from being susceptible to your competition is to build a path to an Exceptional Experience. We are not advocating that you should master all five of the I. C.A.R.E. Principles or all 50 of our supporting concepts. However, we do encourage you to master a few and commit to finding out what level you are currently at. You should absolutely take the online Experience Quotient test. Find your point of origin and then utilize our algorithmic recommendations to move up one level on the Experience hierarchy. Most of us do not grow in quantum leaps; we grow in incremental steps. But think of the tremendous personal development you would achieve in a single year if you could be just one level better.

Again, do not try to use *all* of the Actionables; this is not the way this tool works. Take the Experience Quotient and utilize the customized Action Plan to work on your 12 most identifiable weaknesses and threats. Take on one of the sub-Principles per month, apply the Actionables for that concept, and you will soon find yourself and your organization on the path to the Exceptional Experience and to converting your clients and customers to Ambassadors.

Leave the World Behind

When entering Disney World in Orlando, Florida, you will see a sign above the main entrance passage that reads, "Here you leave Today and enter the world of Yesterday, Tomorrow and Fantasy." This encapsulates what an Experience should be. Whether the client, customer, consumer, or parishioner is walking into a dealership, advisory firm, hotel, restaurant, hospital, retail store, or church, the individual is leaving behind the outside world and entering one that you have created. Are you selling products and services to people—or are you creating an Experience and Ambassadors for your organization? It truly is a choice. Which one are you doing now? And what do you want to be doing in the future?

More than 500 companies were tested in our study of where American companies stand in the hierarchy of the Experience. Are you a part of the 60 percent of companies that are either Average or delivering a Toxic Experience? Or are you a part of the 15 percent that are delivering the Great or Exceptional Experience? Find out where you stand. We encourage you to accept the One Level Challenge, take the test, implement the Actionables, and start your journey to creating an Exceptional Experience for your employees and customers alike.

Go to: www.ExperienceQuotient.com

And begin building today!

The Standard in Relational Service & CX Training

An Executive Coaching, Consulting and Training firm that provides tools, technology and teaching on the ultimate differentiator for your organization...............the Customer Experience!

For more information please visit

www.TheExpInt.com

Or

www.ExperienceQuotient.com

"The Catalyst of the Customer Experience Revolution"

INDEX